A Passion *for* Nature

THOMAS JEFFERSON *and* NATURAL HISTORY

A PASSION *for* NATURE

THOMAS JEFFERSON *and* NATURAL HISTORY

by Keith Thomson

MONTICELLO

THOMAS JEFFERSON FOUNDATION

Monticello Monograph Series

2008

Library of Congress Cataloging-in-Publication Data

Thomson, Keith Stewart.
  A passion for nature : Thomas Jefferson and natural history / Keith Thomson.
      p. cm. -- (Monticello monograph series)
Includes bibliographical references and index.
  ISBN 978-1-882886-26-5 (alk. paper)
  1. Jefferson, Thomas, 1743-1826. 2. Naturalists--Virginia--Biography. 3.
Scientists--Virginia--Biography. 4. Natural history--Virginia. I. Title.

QH31.T47T46 2008
508.092--dc22

                                                                        2008037354

ON THE COVER
The Mockbird from Mark Catesby, *The Natural History of Carolina, Florida and the Bahama Islands*
(London, 1731–43). Courtesy Ewell Sale Stewart Library, The Academy of Natural Sciences.

For photographs and illustrations in this book Thomas Jefferson Foundation is pleased to
acknowledge the following individuals whose work is part of our image collection:
Rick Britton, 12; Peter J. Hatch, 15; Skip Johns, 35; Edward Owen, 10, 68, 70, 99;
Leonard G. Phillips, 23, 33; Jack Robertson, 97; Derek Wheeler, 25; Chad Wollerton, 39.

Designed by Gibson Design Associates
Edited by Sarah Allaback

This book was made possible by support from the
Martin S. and Luella Davis Publications Endowment.

Distributed by
The University of North Carolina Press
Chapel Hill, North Carolina 27515-2288
1-800-848-6224

"Your [letter] … gives me information in the line of Natural history, and … promises political news. The first is my passion, and the last my duty, and therefore both desireable."

—THOMAS JEFFERSON TO HARRY INNES
March 7, 1791

CONTENTS

Map of Virginia from Notes on the State of Virginia *(American Philosophical Society)*

Chapter One

ALBEMARLE

On quiet, still summer mornings when the mists are starting to lift from the woods of central Virginia, and at midday when the fields are shimmering in the heat, one can feel a little of what this rich and varied landscape must have been, two hundred and fifty years ago. To the west, the mountains, dramatic but not intimidating, frame the picture. A turkey vulture soars overhead; the corn is green and dense; the woods are dark and quiet; at dusk the deer will venture into the open to forage. At these times, it is possible briefly to shut out the noise of the modern century and imagine young Thomas Jefferson, roaming his father's farms on horseback, following the progress of the crops and, always, critically observing every minute detail of the nature that surrounded him.

When Jefferson (born 1743) was growing up in Albemarle County, Virginia, in the foothills of the Appalachian Mountains, the land was still mostly wilderness. Everyone, even in towns like Williamsburg and Richmond, lived close to the land. Albemarle County was larger in the 1700s than it is today, having been subdivided since the days when Jefferson roamed it on horseback. Kite-shaped, it reaches along the James River from near Scottsville into the Blue Ridge Mountains.[1] In Jefferson's Virginia, roads were poor and the rivers were all-important for transport and communication. Navigation of the James River for blue-water vessels ended at Richmond. From there, imported goods were moved upstream and crops shipped downstream on smaller craft. For Jefferson, the key river was the Rivanna which runs southeast out of the mountain country, joining the James at Columbia.

Whether duty required him to charm princes (and princesses) in Paris, or to engage in the political hurly-burly of Philadelphia and New York, Jefferson always yearned to be home. He loved Virginia, with its richly varied landscapes, flora, and fauna. All throughout his life, he would never be as happy as there amidst the constantly changing green and gold of the fields, the darkness of the forests,

Portrait of Jefferson by John Trumbull,
1788 (Thomas Jefferson Foundation)

the permanence of the mountains, and the mists that give them their name, the Blue Ridge. Writing from Paris in 1785, the future president of the United States, a connoisseur of fine wines and even more a lover of good books, described himself as "savage enough to prefer the woods, the wilds, and the independence of Monticello, to all the brilliant pleasures of this gay capital … for tho' there is less wealth there, there is more freedom, more ease and less misery."[2]

Home for Thomas Jefferson was first Shadwell, the farm of his father Peter Jefferson, a man whose "education had been neglected"; but being of "strong mind, sound judgment, and eager after information, he read much and improved himself."[3] Peter Jefferson was one of the first to farm in Albemarle County. The Jeffersons were middling members of the Virginia elite, not the richest of them by any means, but Peter Jefferson amassed a major estate and became an important figure in the state and county. He was a successful farmer, land speculator, justice of the peace, and sheriff. He made an enduring mark as a surveyor, a valuable skill in what were essentially frontier lands. Most notably, Peter collaborated with his colleague and neighbor, Joshua Fry, to produce the first map of Virginia. This project in exploration and surveying has interesting echoes in the Lewis and Clark expedition, commissioned by his son half a century later, which started the process of pushing the western frontier to the very edge of the continent. Thomas Jefferson was only fourteen, but already an independent spirit, when his father died, leaving him property and responsibilities.

Jefferson's mother Jane Randolph was the daughter of Isham Randolph of Goochland County. The Randolph family was close to being Virginia aristocracy, and Isham Randolph was well known for his scientific interests and expertise in botany. When the pioneering Philadelphia botanist John Bartram planned a trip into Virginia to collect plants for his London patron, the wealthy merchant Peter Collinson, in 1738, Collinson instructed him to visit Isham Randolph. Bartram stayed with the Randolphs for several days, making botanical excursions into the surrounding country. Randolph guided Bartram to an interesting kind of conifer which Bartram later pronounced "much the finest Arborvitae, surpassing one he had obtained … from Hudson's River." Amusingly, Collinson had advised Bartram to dress his best for this visit, as Quaker plain clothes would make a poor impression. "These Virginians are a very gentle, well-dressed people—and look, perhaps, more at a man's outside than his inside. For these and other reasons, pray go very clean, neat, and handsomely dressed to Virginia. Never mind thy clothes, I will send more another year."[4]

In the mid-1700s, a Virginia farming family, with its entourage of servants and slaves, had to be prepared to be largely self-sufficient. The men had to know all the practical arts: how to build a house, set up a saw pit for lumber, and construct a kiln for burning bricks. They needed to be skilled in nail making, milling, and blacksmithing. The women had to know all the domestic arts, including soap making, spinning and weaving, dyeing, and simple medicine. Both had to train their slaves in their tasks. A great deal of what the family needed had to be taken from the wild environment (grown, or bartered for). Items like sugar, olive oil, oranges and lemons, spices, tea and coffee, some medicines, wines, writing paper, books, dishes and glasses, silver, quality cloth, and livery for the house servants, however, all had to be bought from abroad.

These Virginian landowners prided themselves on being cultivated men and women. Peter Jefferson assembled a library of significant size for its time. It included volumes on subjects from the Latin and Greek classics to works on natural history and animal husbandry. Browsing in this library was surely where Jefferson developed his lifelong love of books. On the death of his father, the library became Jefferson's own. But when Shadwell burned to the ground in early 1770, the library was lost. "I calculate th[e cost o]f t[he b]ooks burned to have been

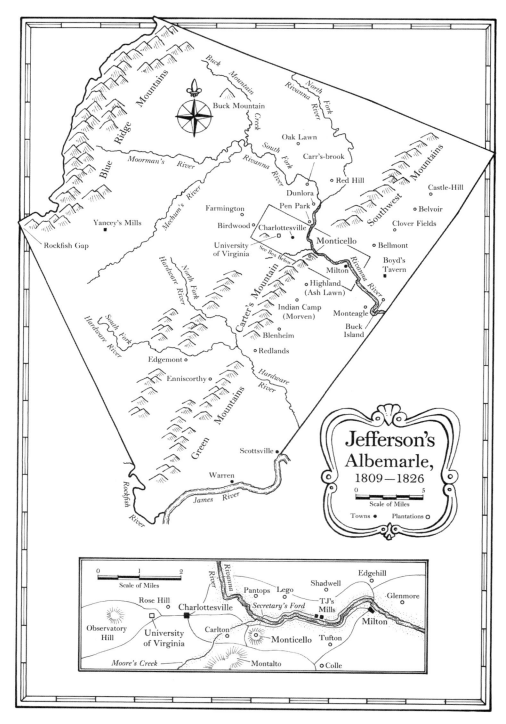

Map of Albemarle County (Thomas Jefferson Foundation)

£200. sterling. Would to god it had been the money[; then] had it never cost me a sigh!" wrote Jefferson.[5]

Farming at Shadwell, as in most of Virginia from the Tidewater to the mountains, was based on tobacco, a crop that sucked the very life out of the land. The common practice was to clear the forest, grow tobacco for three to five years, and then leave the fields to revert to scrub. It would have been a wasteful system, had not land been in plentiful supply. As Jefferson once remarked to George Washington, "we can buy an acre of new land cheaper than we can manure an old one."[6] Tobacco was also demanding of labor, but there was enough for the task— of the roughly half a million souls living in Virginia in 1781, fully half were slaves. Farmers like Jefferson also grew corn, largely for domestic consumption, and that was almost as demanding of the soil as tobacco. By the late 1700s, a variety of factors forced plantation owners to change from growing tobacco to wheat: it was easier to grow, kinder to the land, and there was a strong market for it both in Europe and at home (until the economic crash of 1819).

The indigenous Indian populations of Virginia had long since been decimated by disease, and the remaining bands had been forced much farther west, although traveling groups of Indians (delegations going to and from the capital

"Indian Man in his Summer Dress," from Robert Beverley, The History and Present State of Virginia, *1705 (The Library Company of Philadelphia)*

at Williamsburg) were a familiar—and unthreatening—presence in the county, and Peter Jefferson's Shadwell was one place where they would find an hospitable welcome. The land on which Jefferson was born was already far from a pristine paradise. For millennia the vast forests had been modified by the Indians as they cleared land for their fields, either killing the trees by girdling the bark and then setting fires or by following fires that broke out due to lightning. Most signs of their once extensive settlements and fields had been overgrown when the Europeans began settling Albemarle County. By the 1750s, there was already much disturbed land, abandoned after tobacco farming, as well. In the resulting diversification of habitats, the biological richness of the whole region, from smallest insects to largest forest trees, was on a far greater scale than any European country. In fact there were more different species of native trees in Virginia than in all of Western Europe combined.

The forests by Jefferson's time were a mix of primeval species such as hickory, chestnut, white oak, red oak, post oak, yellow poplar, beech, black walnut, hemlock, and introduced species. Species like Virginia pine, short leaf and loblolly pine, and black locust colonized the more open ground and areas of regrowth, where persimmon, sassafras, and mulberry also flourished. Wild strawberries and grape colonized the open patches. In the spring, the woods were bright with the blossoms of redbud, dogwood, azalea, and Catawba rhododendron. In the fall foliage, black gum, maple, and dogwood provided new bursts of color. Wildflowers were everywhere.

White-tailed deer, beavers, wild turkeys, black bears, raccoons, foxes, woodchucks, skunks, otters, weasels, opossums, squirrels, and chipmunks were common then, as they are today. There were also bobcats, cougars (panthers or catamounts), and wolves. A few buffalo (bison) and even elk (on the high ground) may have survived into the nineteenth century. Today, more than fifty species of mammals can be identified, along with a similar number of amphibians (frogs and salamanders) and some forty species of reptiles, including the rattlesnake. The insect species were beyond counting, but Jefferson personally knew some seventy to a hundred species of birds.

Learning the natural history of his homelands would have been as natural to Jefferson as learning to ride or shoot. He was schooled in the classics (both Latin and Greek) from an early age. At the age of sixteen he attended the College of William and Mary where one of his teachers was William Small. Very much a product of the Enlightenment, Small was a man with broad interests in science and nature, as well as philosophy and the law. "It was my great good fortune, and what probably fixed the destinies of my life that Dr. William Small of Scotland, was then Professor of Mathematics, a man profound in most of the useful branches of science."[7] Jefferson very early became a collector of minerals, plants, animal bones, insects, and fossil shells. Perhaps his most precious collection of all was his library. By all accounts he studied prodigiously—for fifteen hours or more each day—in addition to practicing his violin. At age twenty-five he was already an accomplished lawyer, farmer, and architect with a broad knowledge of science and the works of the great European philosophers and naturalists to go with his intensely personal experiences in the natural laboratory of Albemarle County.

For Jefferson, nature began at home. Like a medieval monastery, every Virginia home had a large garden for vegetables and herbs (both culinary and medicinal). In his *The Natural History of Virginia, or the Newly Discovered Eden*, a piece of promotional literature written to attract Swiss settlers, William Byrd reported on the wealth of crops that were being grown in 1737: "white and red cabbage, turnips, carrots, beets, ... also beautiful cauliflower, chives, artichokes, radish, horseradish, many species of potatoes, also truffles, parsnips ... garlic, smooth, curled and red lettuce, ... spinach ... long asparagus of splendid flavor ... many species of melons ... cucumbers, four spe-

Artichoke, Monticello vegetable garden (Thomas Jefferson Foundation)

cies of pumpkins, simnals, horns, squashes." All of these except the last few were originally imported from Europe.[8] Growing flowers for ornamentation and simple pleasure was more of a luxury, but in many ways it was just as essential—providing for the soul as well as the body. The flower beds and vegetable beds at Shadwell were very neatly laid out in rectangles, each numbered. A sense of order and system in the garden was evidently inculcated in Jefferson at an early age.

In the countryside, the seasons are marked both by the weather and the coming and goings of nature—the first leafing out of the trees, the arrival and departure of migrant birds, planting time, the first flowerings of crop plants and ornamentals, and harvest time. A thousand minor landmarks of the year were evidenced in the lives of animals and plants and all of that, in turn, was reflected in the rhythms of planting and harvesting. Familiarity with the cycles of nature, by everyone from the plantation owner to the lowest slave, was an essential part of the agricultural year. No textbooks or technical manuals were needed. Even illiterate people knew when the signs were right for planting the corn, for hilling the tobacco fields, for putting the ewes to the ram and the cows to the bull, when the hay was ready to be cut, and the apples would be ripe. No farmer could be successful without being a close observer of nature and being surrounded with workers similarly equipped to read the ever-changing signals of the land. Plantation, garden, field, and forest were a textbook of nature for the young Jefferson. He was always a keen and astute observer of everything around him. When he was minister to France, he sent back home notes on everything from agriculture, public gardens, and great estates to the personal habits of the French people. At home, Jefferson tried to ride every day. From the back of a horse one can cover a lot of ground and see a great deal. He collected information and then he tried to use it.

Attitudes toward nature have changed immensely since Jefferson's time. People like Jefferson, and most North Americans, lived in an uneasy balance with the wilderness. Even the most urban of Americans, living in cities like Philadelphia and Boston, were always aware of the wilderness beyond the settlements and of the forests and unpopulated lands to the west full of unknown dangers. Without constant vigilance, the wilderness would take back the land that had so laboriously been tamed. Jefferson's attitude toward nature was not simply that of an admirer (which is what we moderns have become) but of a controller and an improver. As with so much of his character, there were two sides to Jefferson's attitudes toward nature. Many aspects of wild nature, especially landscapes, appealed to his aesthetic side; at heart, he always associated his greatest contentment with closeness to nature. He sought happiness "in an interest or affection in every bud that opens." And he wrote to George Gilmer, "Too many scenes of happiness mingle themselves with all the recollections of my native woods and feilds, to suffer them to be supplanted in my affection by any other."[9]

But Jefferson was always also an intensely practical man. For him, the real nature in which men lived day to day was something to be changed and controlled. Constant work and the application of science, especially the introduction of new plant species such as grasses to improve grazing or fruits, vegetables, and trees for harvesting, would direct and control nature for man's benefit. The strength of the country depended on the successes of agriculture and the provision of food and raw materials, beginning with timber, for industry. That meant harnessing nature and taming it; in turn, that required detailed knowledge and an understanding of what was possible and what was not.

· · ·

From an early age Jefferson became an almost obsessive note-taker and list-maker. It was a habit that stayed with him all his life and is surely one of the keys to his personality. It all began with his fascination for nature in the family farm and garden. As an adult, for forty-eight years, from 1776 to 1824, he collected notes into a Garden Book, which gives us an extraordinary view, not only of what actually happened in the gardens, but of his turn of mind. Its first entries gave details of the garden and woods at Shadwell.

Mar.	30	Purple hyacinth begins to bloom
Apr.	6.	Narcissus and Puckoon [hyacinth] open.
	13.	Puckoon flowers fallen

16.   A bluish colored funnel-formed flower in lowgrounds in bloom

30.   Purple flag blooms. Hyacinth & Narcissus gone.

May 4.   Wild honeysuckle in our woods open.—also the Dwarf flag & Violet

7.   Blue flower in lowgrounds vanished.

11.   The purple flag, Dwarf flag, Violet & wild Honeysuckle still in bloom.

These notes reveal something of Jefferson's knowledge of the wild flowers of Virginia. The bluish flower that he could not identify was almost certainly the Virginia Bluebell, *Mertensia virginica*.

The Garden Book also reveals Jefferson's delight in putting numbers to things and his devotion to anything to do with peas—his favorite vegetable. At Shadwell in 1767 he "sowed a bed of forwardest and a bed of midling peas. 500. of these peas weighed 3oz—18 dwt. about 2500 fill a pint."[10] On (April 24), "forwardest peas of Feb. 20. come to table."[11] Two years later he wrote that "Millar's Gard. Dict. sais that 50. hills of Cucumbers will yield 400. cucumbers a week during the time they are in season, which he sais is 5 week. So that 50 hills will yield 2000, or 1.hill yield 40. cucumbers." In a similar early entry in his Garden Book, he noted the calculation that "8 or 10. bundles of fodder are as much as a horse will generally eat thro' the night. 9 bundles x 130. days = 1170. for the winter. 27 head of cattle convert 65 loads of straw & haulm … into about 300. loads of dung."[12]

Whether at Monticello (where he moved in 1770 after Shadwell burned) or during his many absences on the business of Virginia or the new nation, Jefferson loved to exchange information with others. His letters from Philadelphia and Paris were at their most poignant when he begged for information from home. For example, in 1790, now secretary of state and based in New York, he wrote to his daughter Maria at Monticello: "We had not peas nor strawberries here until the 8th. day of this month. On the same day I heard the first Whip-poor-will whistle. Swallows and martins appeared here on the 21st. of April. When did they appear with you? And when had you peas, strawberries, and whip-poor-wills in

Virginia? Take notice hereafter whether the whip-poor-wills always come with the strawberries and peas."[13] The reply came back that "We had pease the 14 of May and strawberries the 17 of the same month.... As for the martins swallows and whippoorwills I was so taken up with my chickens that I never attended to them...."[14]

A similar exchange followed the next year. He wrote to Maria: "On the 27th. of February, [1791] I saw blackbirds and Robinredbreasts and on the 7th. of this month I heard frogs for the first time this year. Have you noted the first appearance of these things at Monticello? I hope you have, and will continue to note every appearance animal and vegetable which indicates the approach of Spring, and will communicate them to me. By these means we shall be able to compare the climates of Philadelphia and Monticello. Tell me when you have the peas &c. up ... when you shall have the first chickens hatched, when every kind of tree blossoms...".[15] There are some wonderful juxtapositions in these letters. He wants his daughter to record data for him, in part simply for the sake of knowing and keeping records. He also wants to be reminded of home. His requests are also a gentle reminder of the tasks to be undertaken and monitored. Finally, he wants to discover a useful piece of knowledge about the differences between climates of Philadelphia and Monticello—whose seasons turned out to be offset by approximately four weeks.

In addition to records of the vegetable and flower gardens at Monticello, Jefferson kept a Farm Book and a Memorandum Book that recorded the often precarious state of his finances. And from 1776 right up to his death, he kept a Weather Memorandum Book in which he noted temperature, rainfall, barometric pressure, and wind direction. He persuaded friends to keep similar records, instructing James Madison, for example, to take readings at sunrise and four o'clock. He tried to continue this practice when away from Monticello. In Philadelphia, between July 2, 1776, when the Continental Congress first approved the Declaration of Independence and July the fourth when it was signed, the weather was quite mild (especially for a Philadelphia summer). Judging from Jefferson's entries, which are mostly taken in the morning or evening, the temperature ranged no higher than the lower eighties. At night it was in the sixties. There was a gentle southeast breeze, so we can conclude that the signers enjoyed unusually pleasant weather and nothing like the heat and humidity that many popular writers have invented for that occasion. All this record-taking was part of Jefferson's general philosophy that "A patient pursuit of facts, and cautious combination and comparison of them, is the drudgery to which man is subjected by his Maker, if he wishes to attain sure knowledge."[16]

Growing up in the latter-day Eden of mid-eighteenth-century Virginia, where he combined a love of scholarship and a passion for nature with the life of a farmer, Jefferson developed a personal philosophy from which he never wavered throughout his long and extraordinarily accomplished life in the world of politics and government. For Jefferson, knowledge was the key to everything. But knowledge was best when applied directly to useful ends. In contrast to the fashions of our modern academic world, in which pure science and pure knowledge are often thought to be the essential foundation for the development of useful applications, Jefferson believed that one must strive directly for "useful knowledge." In the New World, there was little time for pure abstraction; practical matters were too pressing. This often created something of a dilemma for Jefferson, whose love of philosophy and pure knowledge sometimes conflicted with his drive constantly to find solutions for practical problems—whether in science, in agriculture, or in government. Natural history was not just a hobby for Jefferson, it was central to his world view. Out of his passion for natural history, Jefferson developed the belief that nature is the guide to all that is good and pure and thus must be the basis of a person's education and subsequently their general philosophy. The most useful and satisfying lives, therefore, were those lived close to nature, rather than in cities. He believed that farming and farmers formed the base of a democratic nation of honest, hard-working citizens.

• • •

Although he loved the mountains and lowlands of Virginia, Jefferson spent a great deal of time away from home. After service in the Virginia House of Burgesses (from 1769), Jefferson was elected to the Virginia delegation to the

Second Continental Congress in Philadelphia, where his previous experience in drafting *A Summary View of the Rights of British America* became the foundation for his central authorship of the Declaration of Independence. He served a term as governor of Virginia (1779-1781). From 1784 to 1789 he was minister to France. In 1789 he became secretary of state. He returned to Virginia, as he hoped for good; instead he was elected vice president in 1796, and of course he served as president from 1801 to 1809. Jefferson finally retired to Monticello, which never ceased to be a great work in progress, both in the plantation farms, the gardens, and the house itself. He was then able to devote himself more fully to one of his most ambitious projects: founding, planning, and designing the University of Virginia.

Chapter Two

THE PRACTICAL NATURALIST AT HOME

The geology of Albemarle County, Virginia, is as varied as the landscape. The underlying rocks, ranging from some of the oldest on earth in the mountain belt to the merely 225-million-year-old Triassic sediments in the lower lands, have been deeply weathered, creating soils of good fertility. The Jefferson family properties were concentrated around a ridge of hills reaching to 1,000 feet and more that formed a front range of the Blue Ridge Mountains. This ridge was formed of ancient (575-million-year-old) Catoctin greenstone, a basalt that had originally been formed under the sea before being lifted up in the folding that produced the Appalachians. Near present-day Charlottesville, the Rivanna River has cut through this line of hills; from Shadwell, Jefferson could look across the river and up at land owned by his father. He inherited these forested hilltops, looming over the river, when his father died in 1757. That was the place where, quite early in his life, Thomas Jefferson decided he would one day build his own house. The result was the architectural masterpiece and working plantation of Monticello (little mountain), his home for fifty-six years.

The hill was thickly forested and quite steep even at its 850-foot summit. In 1768, never one for doing things by halves, Jefferson set men not only to clearing trees but also leveling the entire top of his "mountain." A large amount of earth had to be moved before building on the house could begin and the places for a future large vegetable garden and an orchard could be laid out. As usual, Jefferson accounted for every piece of work carefully, even compulsively. He reckoned that a "laborer will grub half an acre to an acre a week of common bushy land in winter." The work was done by hired hands: "the price of grubbing is 24/ pr. Acre in August, and cutting down & cutting up the large timber ready for burning is 16/." In many cases the work was paid for in barter rather than cash: "May 15 (1768) Agreed with mr. Moor that he shall level 250 f. square on the top of the mountain at the

Aerial view of Monticello (Thomas Jefferson Foundation)

N.E. end by Christmas, for which I am to give him 180 bushels of wheat, and 24 bushels of corn, 12 of which are not to be paid till corn comes in."[17] The following winter, Jefferson had a cellar dug for what would become the South Pavilion and, of course, he made more calculations: "four good fellows, a lad and two girls of abt. 16 each in 8½ hours dug in my cellar of mountain clay a place 3 f. deep, 8 f. wide and 16½ f. long = 14⅔ cubic yards ... from this I think a middling hand in 12. hours (including his breakfast) could dig & haul away the earth of 4. cubical yds. in the same soil."[18]

In preparation for the future orchard, the twenty-five-year-old lawyer showed the botanical expertise that he had been developing in the gardens at Shadwell by grafting cherry and walnut "buds" onto different stocks. The following year, he planted out peach stocks on which to graft almonds, apricots, and nectarines, together with pears, cherries, and apples, on the southwest side of the mountain. These were scientifically placed twenty-five feet apart in precisely aligned rows of twelve.

Rarely had anyone felt so passionately about a landscape, and rarely had a life been so intimately bound up with the land and nature, or on so grand a scale. There is an odd contradiction, however, in the fact that the same year that Jefferson began work on his ideal mountain retreat from the rest of the world, he ran for election to the Virginia House of Burgesses and thus launched himself onto a path that led to the presidency and periods of many, many years away from his beloved mountaintop. Monticello was his observatory and his laboratory. Right from the beginning it was a place where he experimented with gardening, farming, and architecture. And it was here that, after the presidency, he put into practice ideas that he had been developing for thirty years while traveling both in Europe and America. It was here that he continued to experiment with new varieties of plants for the garden and farm and to develop new ways of farming.

Although bottomland might have been better for fields, it is easy to see why Jefferson chose the site for his house and plantation. Once the thick oak, chestnut, and hickory forest had been cleared, the soil was deep and quite rich. The views were magnificent. "Of prospect I have a rich profusion and offering itself at every point of the compass. Mountains distant & near, smooth & shaggy, single & in ridges, a little river hiding itself among the hills."[19] A French visitor to Monticello described the house and setting vividly: "Mr. Jefferson's house commands one of the most extensive prospects you can meet with … the mountain on which the house is seated commands all the neighbouring heights as far as the Chesapeake."[20]

Monticello brought out the most lyrical in Jefferson's writing, and it was at its most flowery whenever he was writing to a lady. As he described Monticello to Maria Cosway, the woman with whom he had been engrossed in Paris, the effect was almost excessive: "our own dear Monticello, where has nature spread so rich a mantle under the eye? mountains, forests, rocks, rivers. With what majesty do we there ride above the storms! How sublime to look down into the workhouse of nature, to see her clouds, hail, snow, rain, thunder, all fabricated at our feet! And the glorious Sun, when rising as if out of a distant water, just gilding the tops of the mountains, and giving life to all nature."[21]

This sounds overblown, but the fact is that Monticello does ride above much of the weather as it develops in the Rivanna Valley below.

When Jefferson had finished with it (to the extent that he actually did finish), the apparently natural landscape that surrounded Monticello was, in fact, artfully contrived so that visitors to the house would see virtually nothing of the plantation operations or slave cabins. This effect even extended to the approaches. Jefferson drove in on a long road along the north side of the property, set within a swath of the old forest trees.

Margaret Bayard Smith wrote of her visit in 1809: "we began to ascend this mountain, still as we rose I cast my eyes around, but could discern nothing but

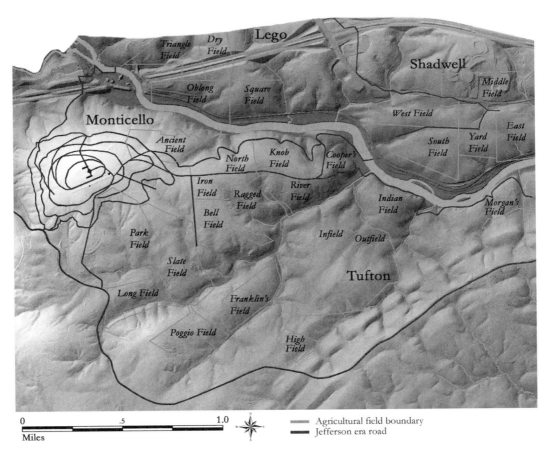

Map of agricultural fields and roads surrounding Monticello (Thomas Jefferson Foundation)

untamed woodland, after a mile's winding upwards we saw a field of corn, but the road was still wild and uncultivated."[22] She did eventually get to see the slaves and the working part of the estate and was less than impressed. Francis Calley Gray, visiting in 1814, even thought that, on the drive up the mountain, "the forest had evidently been abandoned to nature; some of the trees were decaying from age, some were blasted, some uprooted by the wind."[23] George Ticknor, the following year, said that the "ascent of this steep, savage hill was as pensive and slow as Satan's ascent to Paradise."[24] But when each visitor reached the top, all had the reaction reported by Margaret Bayard Smith: "…at last we reached the summit, and I shall never forget the emotion the first view of this sublime scenery excited."

Once the trees had been cleared, Jefferson set out to create a refined and picturesque version of nature. He carefully surrounded the house with extensive gardens and parkland that both separated the house from the plantation beyond and linked them into one whole. A special feature of the grounds, a result of building on a hilltop, was the series of concentric roads, the "Roundabouts" with interconnecting diagonals at varying degrees of slope (one in ten, one in twenty). To the north and west of the house, he planned his "Grove," created by cutting out "superabundant plants" and opening up vistas. Here, he noted to himself, he would "thin the trees, cut out stumps … cover the whole with grass. intersperse Jessamine, honeysuckle, sweetbriar, and even hardy flowers which may not require attention. keep it in deer, rabbits, Peacocks, Guinea poultry, pigeons, etc. let it be an asylum for hares, squirrels, pheasants, partridges, and every other wild animal (except those of prey) … procure a buck-elk, to be, as it were, monarch of the wood; but keep him shy … a buffalo might be confined also … benches or seats of rock or turf."[25]

In the end, the deer park was established separately, to the south of the house. As the slave Isaac Jefferson recalled, the deer park was "two or three miles round and fenced in with a high fence, twelve rails double-staked and ridered." The deer were fed at sunup and sundown "called 'em up and fed 'em wid corn … gave 'em salt; got right gentle; come up and eat out of your hand." If Jefferson heard hunters near the park he "used to go down thar wid his gun and order 'em out."[26]

Jefferson's deer park was interesting for the fact that in 1776 he actually had to purchase two deer—an adult for twenty shillings and a fawn for twelve shillings and six pence. Evidently deer were then not the common pest that they are today, probably because they were aggressively hunted by people and by wolves. Jefferson never did get his elk, although Byrd had reported in 1737 that "one finds many elk in the woods ... the horns are of terrible size, their meat is good, and the skin is pleasant for many things."[27] Of other animals, Isaac reported that Jefferson kept rabbits, which were often eaten.

Although there had been some changes as civilization encroached, the wild-life of these upland forests was still very much as Robert Beverley had reported at the beginning of the eighteenth century: "they, have the Advantage of Wild Turkeys, of an incridible Bigness, Pheasants, Partridges, Pigeons, and an Infinity of small Birds, as well as Deer, Hairs, Foxes, Raccoons, Squirrels, Possums. And upon the Frontier Plantations, they meet with Bears, Panthers, Wild-Cats, Elks, Buffaloes, and Wild Hogs, which yield Pleasure, as well as Profit to the Sports-man."[28] Isaac Jefferson reported that, "there were no wildcats at Monticello; some lower down at Buck Island. Wolves so plenty that they had to build pens round black peoples' quarters and pen sheep in `em to keep the wolves from catching them. But they killed five or six of a night in the winter season; come and steal in the pens at night. When the snow was on the groun', you could see the wolves in gang runnin' and howlin', same as a drove of hogs; made the deer run up to the feedin' place many a night ... they raised many sheep and goats at Monticello ... The woods and mountains was often on fire. Isaac has gone out to help put out the fire. Everybody would turn out from Charlottesville and everywhere; git in the woods and sometimes work all night fightin' the fire."

• • •

The first building at Monticello was the small brick pavilion of one room, for which the cellar had been dug in 1769. This structure was designed to become the south pavilion of the eventual house. Jefferson had to move here when Shadwell burned down early in 1770. When he took his new bride, Martha Wales Skelton, to live at Monticello two years later, they squeezed very uncomfortably into this one-room house until the main house could be occupied.

Jefferson always built in brick. Shadwell had been a timber frame house on brick foundations and it had burned easily. Jefferson rejected such timber houses as "ugly, uncomfortable, and happily more perishable" than the huts the "the poorest people build … of logs, laid horizontally in pens, stopping the interstices with mud. These are warmer in winter, and cooler in summer, than the more expensive constructions of scantling and plank."[29] Clay for bricks was in plentiful supply on the estate. Being on a mountaintop had one disadvantage, however; there was a terrible shortage of water which slowed the brick-making process. Jefferson noted that "a bed of mortar which makes 2000. bricks takes 6. hhds. of water."[30]

As an architect, Jefferson was very strongly influenced by the sixteenth-century Italian Andrea Palladio, whose ideas of classic line and proportion and use of columns and porticos can be seen in literally hundreds of eighteenth-century buildings across Europe. As adopted by Jefferson, it was a unique and powerful style. As time went by, the house was extended and rebuilt to accommodate Jefferson's growing family; his older daughter Martha Jefferson Randolph lived there with her husband Thomas Mann Randolph and eleven surviving children. In his designing and later rebuilding of Monticello—grafting onto it the first dome on any house in America—Jefferson articulated all his ideas about design, form, and function.

With the family, hired hands, and up to two hundred slaves, the estate was, in effect, a small self-sufficient village. The house became a showcase for Jefferson's natural history specimens, his paintings, and his library.[31] The galleried front entrance hall, with its tall glass doors and calendar clock, was where Jefferson displayed his extensive collections. In 1816, Baron de Montlezun noted in his journal that the room was essentially a museum. In fact, Jefferson often used it as a kind of classroom to entertain and educate his visitors. It was here that Jefferson's collection of huge fossil remains (described in Chapter Five) was displayed. He had the frontal bone and the upper and lower jaws of a mastodon, plus "a mammoth's tusk and an elephant's with a tooth of the latter to show how much it differs from those of the mammoth; the latter being conical and indicating a carnivore, while the other, flat and streaked at the crown, a fructivore."[32] Standing in the hall today, one can almost hear Jefferson lecturing his guest. The walls were hung with various antlers including splendid sets from elk and moose. There was the stuffed head of a mountain sheep from the Lewis and Clark expedition. Jefferson also had many dried animal specimens and others in jars, preserved in spirits of wine. Jefferson's favorite American bird was the mockingbird and he kept a tame one in his bedroom-study. It would sing, sit on his shoulder, and even take food from his mouth.

Along with many paintings and sculptures, Jefferson displayed Indian artifacts including "an Indian painting representing a battle; it is on buffalo hide, about five feet square. There are four lines of warriors. On each line there are horses; painted red and green opposite each other, as are the warriors, armed and dressed in the manner of savages." There was a "Map, also on buffalo hide … (representing) the course of the Missouri." There were Indian stone carvings, "a little Indian hatchet … in the form of a pipe; a figure of an animal in the same stone; various petrifactions; bows, arrows and a host of objects made by the Indians … a European coat of mail which those who fought with the Indians used in the early wars." In addition to the claw of a western brown (grizzly) bear, Jefferson displayed many other items that had been brought back by Lewis and Clark from the great West in 1806, including skins, "bows and arrows, poisoned spears, peace pipes, moccasins, etc with various articles of clothing and kitchen utensils of the Mandans and other nations of the Missouri … plus petrifications, crystallizations, minerals, shells etc."[33]

These natural history collections were displayed open to view in a way that some visitors thought rather untidy, others found impressive. In any case, they were not there simply to decorate the house and to impress (or even teach); they were a constant reminder to Jefferson of the things that mattered to him most— nature, the exploration and possession of the western lands, and the enigma of the Indians. Unfortunately, most of these important collections were dispersed after Jefferson's death.

The Mockbird from Mark Catesby, The Natural History of Carolina, Florida and the Bahama Islands *(Ewell Stewart Library, Academy of Natural Sciences)*

Elk antlers, circa 1804–5 (University of Virginia)

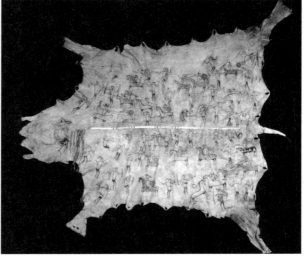

Mandan buffalo robe, circa 1798 (Peabody Museum of Archaeology and Ethnology, Harvard University)

Just as important to Jefferson as the material objects of nature and various human cultures was the world of knowledge and ideas contained inside his vast collection of books. In his lifetime, Jefferson owned or created three major libraries. After the library at Shadwell that he inherited from his father burned with the house in 1770, he promptly began to assemble a new library at Monticello. This became, as Jefferson said, a "statesman's library," with the "best chosen collection of its size probably in America, and containing a great mass of what is most rare and valuable, and especially of what relates to America."[34] When he was forced by debt to sell it to the nation in 1783 there were 3,200 titles (over 6,000 volumes). This library was not just the result of a book collector's hobby. The list of subjects represented was breathtaking—from the ancient classics to modern law and philosophy, gardening to the arts of war, brewing to naval architecture, anatomy and medicine to European history.[35] It was a library worthy of a great university and certainly without parallel in America. Its breadth is a testimony to an extraordinary intellect—always curious, always learned, always intensely practical. Significantly, the largest collection in the library was of books on science, some eight hundred in all (twenty-five percent).[36]

History tended to repeat itself with Jefferson's collections. His father's library burned. Short of money, he sold his "great library" to the nation to replace the one burnt by the British in 1814. Then a fire at the Library of Congress in 1851 destroyed more than half of those books. Jefferson was a man who, as he famously said, could not live without books. Having sold his "great library," he set about building a third. At his death, most of this collection was bequeathed to the University of Virginia, and much of it was lost in a fire there in 1895.

Jefferson was never satisfied with Monticello, always tearing down and building up the main house, as well as trying different combinations in the farm and gardens. Then, in 1806, while he was still president and with Monticello still not finished, he began work on a second house. If Monticello was his magisterial masterpiece, his octagonal house at Poplar Forest was pure magic. Oddly, while Monticello was on a mountain site, Poplar Forest was set in a rather more conventional landscape and not sublime except in the inspiration of the architecture.

It was a strange choice to be his summer retreat; one wonders whether, in part, Jefferson wanted to build Poplar Forest as an exercise in pure architectural form and, like Monticello, another experiment in merging a house seamlessly into the landscape.

Chapter Three

Naturalist, Gardener, Farmer

It was not until after he had retired from the presidency that Jefferson was able to concentrate on making Monticello's house and gardens just as he wanted them and to express in practical terms his knowledge and love of natural history. Jefferson's philosophy for designing an estate was, typically, full of contrasts. As already noted, the overall impression he wanted to create was of a natural setting, although to do that required making a great deal of change in the unruly nature actually present on his mountain. The working vegetable gardens, orchards, vinery, and experimental plots, on the other hand, were the opposite of romantic and disordered. Here nature was subdued into neat lines and squares. Similarly, his plantations were strictly managed and divided into farms of equal size, each with similar fields.

The initial processes of reshaping the site at Monticello continued for several years after 1770. In 1772 we have a typical example of Jefferson's habit of making little detailed calculations and experimenting with new techniques—here use of a two-wheeled wheelbarrow, compared with the standard one-wheeled version: "Julius Shard fills the two-wheeled barrow in 3. minutes and carries it 30. yds. in 1½ minutes more. now this is four loads of the common barrow with one wheel. so that suppose the 4. loads put in the same time viz. 3. minutes, 4. trips will take 4 x 1½ minutes = 6' which added to 3' filling is = 9' to fill and carry the same earth which was filled & carried in the two-wheeled barrow in 4½'. from a trial I made with the same two-wheeled barrow

The Grove, Monticello, 1995 (Thomas Jefferson Foundation)

I found that a man would dig & carry to the distance of 50. yds 5. cubical yds of earth in a day of 12. hours length."[37]

One of the most important first stages in starting work at Monticello was to establish a vegetable garden. That was far more important than thinking about any kind of ornamental flower beds, not just because he and his family had to be fed but because Jefferson always preferred the practical and useful to the decorative. Even as the foundations for the house were being dug, Jefferson had begun the creation of a huge vegetable garden that eventually would be carved out of the hillside as one great terrace—a hanging garden—between the long lane of mulberry trees with its quarters for the house slaves and workers (Mulberry Row) to the north and the orchard to the south below. Originally the garden was 668 feet long and 80 feet wide, with triangular ends. Later Jefferson had it extended to a rectangle one thousand feet long, encompassing two acres, and planned for it to be subdivided into twenty-four neat rectangular beds. In 1809, the whole garden was protected by a ten-foot fence with palings set close enough that a rabbit could not get through. On the downhill side it was supported by a dry-stone wall against which were grown his favorite "Marseilles" variety of fig. Halfway along the wall he built a raised pavilion where he could sit and read and survey his lands all the way over to Tufton, another of the farms that he had inherited from his father. Between the vegetable garden and the orchard were Jefferson's plots for grapes and soft fruit. Altogether, a wide variety of fruits and nuts was grown: cherries, peaches, apples, persimmons, pecans, strawberries, raspberries, and gooseberries. Jefferson was particularly keen on promoting the pecan tree, which he was one of the first to recognize as being a species distinct from the white walnut.

Jefferson had strong views on diet, believing with Dr. Benjamin Rush that one should mostly eat vegetables, treating meat "as a condiment for the vegetables."[38] Mary Randolph advised in her cookbook, *The Virginia House-wife*, that in a Virginia kitchen of the day vegetables were to be cooked until just tender, no more."[39] Jefferson noted with dismay that in Virginia "the poorer people attended to neither [vegetables nor fruits], living principally on milk and animal diet. This is the more inexcusable, as the climate requires indispensably a free use of vegetable

Monticello vegetable garden (Thomas Jefferson Foundation)

food, for health as well as comfort, and is very friendly to the raising of fruits."[40] Jefferson's disapproval of a heavy meat diet was reinforced when he first went to London and observed the natives in their homes. He slyly reported to Abigail Adams that "it must be the quantity of animal food eaten by the English which renders their character insusceptible of civilization. I suspect it is in their kitchens and not in their churches that their reformation must be worked...."[41]

Jefferson's scheme for the vegetable garden for the year 1812 was recorded in the Garden Book.[42] Plantings in the twenty-four square plots were to be arranged in three groups. At the western end, were the "fruits" including beds of asparagus, peas (Leadman's dwarf), snap beans, haricot beans, cucumbers, melons, peppers, "tomatas," okra, artichokes, and squashes. Root vegetables like carrots, salsify, beets, garlic, leeks, and onion were in the middle beds. At the eastern end were the leaf vegetables: scallions, nasturtiums, lettuce, endive, "terragon," celery, spinach, sorrel,

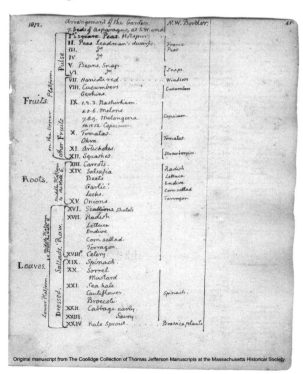

mustard, sea kale, cauliflower, broccoli, and cabbages. Beans and black-eyed peas were also a field crop in the farm, as were several different kinds of potatoes (long, round, Indian, Irish). From Jefferson's meticulous note keeping in his Garden Book and Farm Book, we know that he experimented with some 330 different varieties of vegetables. He grew nearly ninety varieties of peas and beans at one time or another. Peas were his favorite vegetable of all. According to family accounts there was a long-standing competition each spring among the local landowners as to who could bring a dish of peas to table first. With his warm

Planting Scheme for 1812 from the Garden Book (Massachusetts Historical Society)

south-facing terraced garden and his constant experimentation, Jefferson was well placed to win these competitions. But usually the race went to his neighbor, George Divers. On the one occasion when he actually did win, Jefferson decided not to announce the fact for fear of disappointing his old friend.

At Monticello, Jefferson became the consummate practical naturalist and scientist, putting all his knowledge and love of natural history into useful applications and constantly trying out new plant varieties. The old favorite varieties of everything, from peas to peaches and cucumbers to carrots, were constantly tested against those sent to him by his many friends and by professional plantsmen. They regularly sent him seeds, roots, and cuttings of new things that might interest him. He, in turn, would pass on to his friends varieties that he had found useful. After meeting Andre Thouin, superintendent of the Jardin des Plantes in Paris, he exchanged plants and seeds with him for twenty-three years. Among many such correspondents on botanical matters, at home and abroad, was Madame Noailles de Tessé, a cousin of General Lafayette, to whom he once admitted that "I rarely ever planted a flower in my life," having preferred always to plant trees and, of course, his precious vegetable garden. But he went on to tease her by saying that he thought he would now "become a florist." He introduced several new species of plants from the Old World, including the olive tree and African upland (dry) rice. The natural history of the garden was as important to Jefferson as the natural history of the native forests. Like any good scientist, Jefferson kept track of the failures as well as the successes, and no variety, even a favorite, was allowed room if it failed to match up against some new kind. He used his garden plots to try some of the plants discovered by the Lewis and Clark expedition in the American West, both from the dry plains and the cold, wet lands beyond the "Great Stoney Mountains."[43]

A relatively weak "small beer," brewed from local hops and barley, was first made at Monticello under the supervision of Jefferson's wife, Martha. After 1812, Jefferson took on an English brew master, Joseph Miller, a prisoner of war. Wine had to be imported, however. Jefferson grew grapes, for which the climate at Monticello (hot summers, cold winters) was suitable if unpredictable, but the cultivation of vineyards on Virginia's different soils was then still variable. An Italian wine maker, Phillipo Mazzei, spent some years trying to get a vineyard established, but eventually failed.[44] Growing grapes for wine had always been difficult. In commenting on earlier failures, Robert Beverley noted in 1705 that: "The Pine-Tree and Fir are naturally very noxious to the Vine; and the Vine is observed never to thrive, where it is any ways influenced by them. Now, all the lower Parts of their Rivers naturally produce these Trees; insomuch, that if a Man clear the Land there, of the Wood, he will certainly find that the Pine is the first Tree that will grow up again, tho' perhaps there was not a Pine in that Spot of Ground before. Again; the Vine thrives best on the Sides of Hills, Gravelly Ground, and in the Neighbourhood of fresh Streams. But the Experiments that have been made of Vineyards, both in *Virginia* and *Carolina*, have not only been near the malignant Influence of the Salt-Water, but also upon the low Lands, that are naturally subject to the Pine."

Any eighteenth-century garden included a multitude of culinary herbs; lavender, sage, marjoram, thyme, tarragon, rosemary, chamomile, and mint were staples. Herbs were also grown for their medicinal properties, and the blacks were often more skilled in the use of medicinal herbs than their white masters. The slaves also had their own gardens, and Jefferson would buy vegetables from them, presumably when his own supplies were short. Record books show that they sold him cucumbers, simelines (pattypan squash), peaches, watermelons and musc melons, cabbages, potatoes, "a mess of salad & sprouts," "greens and lettuce," strawberries, and dried apples. The household purchased large numbers of chickens and eggs from the slaves. In the week August 25 to September 1, 1805, for example, they bought 26 chickens and 186 eggs (they paid around six pence for a chicken and nine pence for a dozen eggs).[45] While rearing chickens was the slaves' business, the Jefferson grandchildren raised ducks and geese.

After he retired from the presidency, Jefferson set to work on creating a major pleasure garden. He designed it in an English style, rather than the older kind of garden with formal flower beds and straight-line vistas. His design for the west side of the house included sinuous walks and informal plantings. There was a long winding path around the lawn, set about by curving borders and oval flower beds. All the grounds were planted with his favorite ornamental trees, such as *Chionanthus virginica*, the fringe tree (also a favorite of George Washington). One of the oval flower beds near the house was devoted entirely to the only plant that was ever named for Jefferson (Appendix A). This was the twinleaf or *Jeffersonia diphylla. Jeffersonia* is now a relatively rare woodland plant in Virginia, preferring damp, alkaline soils. It was probably first collected by the Philadelphia botanist and collector John Bartram, who for many years had explored the east coast on the continent for species suitable for cultivation

Twinleaf, Jeffersonia diphylla
(Thomas Jefferson Foundation)

and was responsible for sending many new species to his English patron Peter Collinson.[46] The plant was first described scientifically by Linnaeus (in his *Species Plantarum* of 1753), who named it *Podophyllum diphyllum*. His dried specimen was noted as having been obtained from Collinson and thus probably came from Bartram. The Philadelphia botanist Benjamin Smith Barton worked out that it was different from a *Podophyllum* and established the name *Jeffersonia*. At a meeting of the American Philosophical Society, Barton said: "I beg leave to observe to you, in this place, that in imposing upon this genus the name of Mr. Jefferson, I have had no reference to his political characters, or to his reputation for general science, and for literature. My business was with his knowledge of natural history … equalled by few persons in the United States."[47]

• • •

Jefferson's estates included not only the land inherited from his father but also the estates (and many debts) of his father-in-law, John Wales. From Monticello he controlled farms at Tufton, Shadwell, Pouncey's, and Lego in Albemarle County and Poplar Forest, Tomahawk, and Bear Creek in Bedford

County. In all there were some 10,000 acres, much of which was leased to tenant farmers, all of whom were expected to hew very closely to Jefferson's rules and principles for farming. He grew a great deal of wheat, although in the early years he needed to plant tobacco plantation style, as well, because it brought a higher profit even though it was bad for the land. The estate at Monticello itself included about a thousand acres. Jefferson's fields and experimental plots were set out on the southeast side of the mountain, along a ridge that extends down to the Rivanna River. The farms at Shadwell, Tufton, Lego, and Pouncey's brought the total in Albemarle County to about 5,500 acres, of which less than one thousand was under cultivation. At Monticello itself, perhaps only one to two hundred acres of land were in active cultivation at any one time. A fair proportion of the property was in old fields that had been abandoned to re-growth of pine and black locust. Although he had overseers and tenant farmers in place, Jefferson personally supervised all his lands—Monticello, Lego, Shadwell, and Tufton. "From breakfast, or noon at the latest, to dinner, I am mostly on horseback .... which I find healthful to my body...."[48] These excursions were not for pleasure or health alone; he toured the fields and woods and went down to check on his flour mills on the Rivanna. He followed the same practice at Poplar Forest, and it was one of his eccentricities that, as he rode, he sang out loud.

Jefferson was always trying new ideas. He did not plant heavily with boxwood in the pleasure garden, as typical estates of the period did, and for the orchards and fruit plots he constantly tried different species for living fences (hedges). He had success with cedar and holly, but most of those hedges were made with varieties of American hawthorn. In one of the typical speculative calculations that so engaged his mind, especially when he was marooned in Philadelphia or Washington, he had his son-in-law Thomas Mann Randolph make some measurement on the possibility of using the peach orchard as a source of firewood. "your experiment ... proves my speculation practicable, as it shews that 5. acres of peach trees at 21. feet apart will furnish dead wood enough to supply a fire place through the winter, and may be kept up at the trouble of only planting about 70. peach stones a year. Suppose this extended to 10. fireplaces, it comes to 50. acres of ground, 5000 trees, and the replacing of about 700 of them annually … when I indulge myself in these speculations, I feel with redoubled ardor my desire to return home….”[49]

In addition to cash crops, the farms had to produce corn, peas (probably related to modern “black-eyed peas,” which are not a true pea), and potatoes for the support of the extended household of family, hired workers, and slaves. Somewhere between five hundred and one thousand bushels of corn were consumed a year, and often Jefferson had to buy supplies. Tobacco was the big moneymaker in Virginia, and Jefferson depended on it as the main crop for income until about 1793. But not only was it bad for the soil, it was extremely demanding in terms of slave labor. Jefferson, like George Washington, had long since worked out that holding large numbers of slaves was uneconomical. While they were essential for working the plantations, slaves were also young and old dependents who had to be supported. If this seems a liberal sentiment, it should be noted that the children began their working life at the age of eight to ten. And, in a typical contradiction, Jefferson considered owning female slaves a particular economic boon: “I consider a woman who brings a child every two years as more profitable than the best man of the farm. what she produces is an addition to capital, while his labors disappear in mere consumption.”[50]

Indian corn (maize) was almost as hard on the land as tobacco. Jefferson wrote: “The Highlands where I live have been cultivated about 60. years … The culture was tobacco and Indian corn as long as they would bring enough to pay the labour … After 4. or 5. years rest they would bring good corn again and in double that time perhaps good tobacco. Then they would be exhausted by a second series of tobacco and corn.”[51] Both Jefferson and Washington (another very thoughtful farmer) turned to growing wheat, for which there was a ready market. Many farmers alternated wheat and corn in their fields, but that also soon exhausted the upland soils. Instead, Jefferson carefully followed developments in European farming, especially the rotation of crops that was being preached by Arthur Young in England. The principle of this lay in planting crops that would allow the land to recover its fertility while lying fallow. Legume crops, such as clover and peas, actually increase soil fertility because (as is now known) bacteria associated with their roots take nitrogen from the atmosphere and covert it to useful biomass. In his typical fashion, Jefferson's first plans for crop rotations involved an elaborate eight-year cycle for eight fields rotating in turn: wheat and (fall) fallow; peas and corn thinly interplanted; wheat and (fall) fallow; potatoes and corn interplanted; rye and (fall) fallow; clover; clover; clover.[52] As with so many of Jefferson's paper calculations, this was impractical. He devised a six-year plan, but by 1798 he had put in practice a simple three-year rotation: "one year of wheat & two of clover in the stronger fields, or two of peas in the weaker, with a crop of Indian corn & potatoes between every other rotation … under this easy course of culture, aided with some manure, I hope my fields will recover their pristine fertility…."[53]

Another of Jefferson's innovations was contour ploughing, championed both by him and by Thomas Mann Randolph. The result was improved soil conservation, particularly important on the steep slopes around Monticello. And, of course, Jefferson also invented an improved design for an iron plough moldboard that was superior to traditional wooden ploughs.

Chapter Four

An American Man of Science

Thomas Jefferson was only thirty-two when he went to Philadelphia to join the Virginia delegation to the Continental Congress as its youngest member. A year later, he became one of the authors of the Declaration of Independence. We should perhaps not be surprised. This was the man who at the age of twenty-five had planned and designed Monticello, laid out its estates, and supervised its construction. He was already a farmer, an architect, a lawyer, a legislator, and a political theorist. Above all, Jefferson was a scientist, although that term was not then in use. In Philadelphia, Jefferson left the intellectual world defined by the College of William and Mary and was thrown into company with the great American scientists of the day, starting with Benjamin Franklin.[54] Four years later, he was made a member of the American Philosophical Society, the first society of its kind in America and soon to rival the Royal Society in London as a focus of scientific discovery and progress.

Jefferson's scientific interests were exceptionally broad, but they began and ended with natural history which, as he once wrote, was his passion.[55] His love of botany, in particular, was unbounded: "Botany I rank with the most valuable sciences, whether we consider its subjects as furnishing the principal subsistence of life to man and beast,

Benjamin Franklin (Ewell Stewart Library, Academy of Natural Sciences, Philadelphia)

refreshments from our orchards, the adornment of our flower borders, shade and perfume for our groves, materials for our buildings, or mendicants for our bodies." In the eighteenth century, "natural history" meant something more specific than it does today. What we call "science" was then divided into two streams: natural history and natural philosophy. The term "history" was used to mean information— in this case, the discovery, description, and identification of organisms and the organizing of data about the natural world. Natural history was the "who?" and "what?" of science, notably botany, zoology, and mineralogy. Natural philosophy was concerned with the "how?" and "why?" of nature. Its subject matter was the physical sciences and experimentation rather than observation. Natural philosophy therefore included physics (once called experimental philosophy), dynamics (mechanics), astronomy, and chemistry. It involved the discovery of theories as well as facts, and the principles, causations, and laws behind material phenomena.[56]

Whether in natural history or natural philosophy, one of the consequences, and also a cause, of the American Revolution was intellectual—a striving for intellectual independence. Before the war, Americans were almost wholly dependent upon European sources for their literature, philosophy, arts, and science. For example, in the great library that Jefferson created after 1770, few of his pre-1800 books in natural history were written by Americans. Geology, anthropology, mineralogy, zoology, botany—even basic geography—were still taught by European-trained scholars and learned through reading European books. American colleges necessarily inclined to Europe for all things intellectual. Even when Jefferson founded the University of Virginia, he mostly saw to the hiring of European scholars as professors. An American scholarly-professorial class had yet to emerge. In colonial America and in the early decades of the young Republic, despite the efforts of teachers like William Small at the College of William and Mary, many matters seemed more pressing than the pursuit of natural history or natural philosophy.

Jefferson and his colleagues set about developing a uniquely American culture, and the American Philosophical Society in Philadelphia was central to that enterprise. In science, a cadre of remarkable men grew up in and around the Philosophical Society. It had been founded by Franklin in 1743, following a proposal of the botanist John Bartram, but it quickly ran out of steam. Then, in 1766, a new surge of patriotic feeling led to the founding of the American Society for Promoting Useful Knowledge, with a focus on developing and promoting new approaches to agriculture and manufacture. In 1769 the two organizations merged and suddenly there was a critical mass of people to carry things forward; the timing was also right. Between 1780 and 1810, the Society and its publications became the principal voice for science in America. Jefferson became its president in 1789.

Jefferson had joined a remarkable group of men; their devotion to finding ways of turning information into "useful knowledge" fitted his personal philosophy exactly. John Bartram, for example, established a thriving plantsman's business just across the river from Philadelphia. He supplied American botanical specimens to collectors in Europe and brought many European species into cultivation in America.[57] His son William followed in his footsteps, making many important discoveries and writing what Jefferson considered to be one of the classics of American exploration: *Travels Through North and South Carolina, Georgia, East and West Florida, the Cherokee Country, the Extensive Territories of the Muscogulges or Creek Confederacy, and the Country of the Chactaws (1791)*.

In addition to the Bartrams, another Philadelphian, Bernard McMahon, was a major influence on Jefferson as a botanist and gardener, both through his commercial work as a plantsman, sharing seeds and plants with Jefferson, and with his book *The American Gardener's Calendar* (1806). Another very practical natural scientist was William Hamilton, a wealthy Philadelphian who had a six-hundred-acre estate, The Woodlands, where he also experimented with new varieties. Other prominent, more academic, botanists included the Frenchman André Michaux, author of *Flora Boreali-Americana* (*The Flora of North America*, 1803) and *History of the Forest Trees of North America* (1811).

The leading American scholar of natural history was Benjamin Smith Barton of the University of Pennsylvania who wrote the nation's first textbooks of both anthropology and botany (*New Views of the Origin of the Tribes and Nations of America*, 1797; the incomplete *Flora Virginica*, 1812; and *Elements of Botany, or Outlines of the Natural History of Vegetables*, 1803). He was also the editor of

Caspar Wistar, portrait by Thomas Sully, 1830 (Ewell Stewart Library, American Philosophical Society)

Charles Willson Peale, self-portrait, circa 1795 (Independence National Historical Park)

Benjamin Smith Barton (Ewell Stewart Library, Academy of Natural Sciences)

Philadelphia Medical and Physical Journal.[58] Other important American works published around 1800 included John Randolph's *A Treatise on Gardening* (1793); John Shecut's *Flora Carolinensis* (1806); Frederick Pursh's *Flora Americae Septentrionalis* (1814); and Muhlenberg's *Catalogus Plantarum Americae Septentrionalis* (1813).

Apart from these botanists, four other colleagues with whom Jefferson shared interests were the great physician Benjamin Rush; the astronomer, inventor, mathematician, and surveyor David Rittenhouse; the anatomist Caspar Wistar; and the extraordinary artist and showman Charles Willson Peale. Peale was curator of the American Philosophical Society's collections and founder in 1786 of America's first natural history museum. All these men were influential with Jefferson in leading the development of the sort of natural science that would serve the new nation best.

• • •

After an all-too-brief, idyllic period at home in Virginia—building his house, establishing his farms, starting a family—personal tragedy struck in 1782 when Jefferson's wife Martha died. The loss may have contributed to his willingness to take on the post of minister to France and to leave Monticello (and two of his surviving daughters) for Paris. Intellectually, Paris suited him well. He approved of the developing revolutionary politics and, as in Philadelphia, reveled in the intellectual company, which included many of the great natural scientists of the day like Georges Louis Leclerc, Comte de Buffon, and his associate Louis-Jean-Marie d'Aubenton, whom we will meet in the next chapter.

True to form, Jefferson did not stick to the gilded salons of Paris. In 1787 he made a long journey through France and Italy, taking careful note of things—from wine and cheese making, to canals and methods of ploughing—that might be of benefit to America. He became convinced, for example, that olive trees could be grown at home, removing the necessity of importing olive oil, a precious commodity (especially for those addicted, like Jefferson, to French cuisine), and providing a benefit for slaves and the poor. The tour became an extended "field trip." He seems to have missed nothing, even making notes on the cause of the apparent color of the sea (reflection from the sky): "I do not remember to have seen assigned anywhere, the cause." Everywhere, he delighted in the scenery and natural history. At Albenga, Italy, he sounded a little wistful. "If any person wished to retire from their acquaintance, to live absolutely unknown, and yet in the midst of physical enjoyments, it should be in some of the little villages of this coast, where air, earth and water concur to offer what each has most precious. Here are nightingales, beccaficas, ortolans, pheasants, partridges, quails, a superb climate … The earth furnishes wine, oil, figs, oranges, and every production of the garden in every season."[59]

Jefferson took a special interest in the culture of rice. He wanted to know whether the superior quality of Italian rice was due to the machinery used to hull the rice (it was not). "It is a difference in the species of grain, of which the government of Turin is so sensible, that, as I was informed, they prohibit the exportation of rough rice on pain of death." The Carolinas were the main rice growing region of America, using lowland strains that grew in marshland. But that meant that the workers were ravaged by malaria. In Italy they grew an upland, or dry rice, originating in Africa, the cultivation of which involved a much healthier environment. Capital offense or not, Jefferson wanted seeds to take home. "I have taken measures however for obtaining a quantity of it, which I think will not fail, and I bought on the spot a small parcel which I have with me." He smuggled the seeds out in his coat pocket and planted a trial field of upland rice at Monticello.[60]

Soon after returning home to Monticello, Jefferson was presented with a new scientific problem. A terrible insect pest was decimating wheat fields on Long Island. On the assumption that it had been imported by mercenary troops during the war, it was called the Hessian fly. (In fact, the Hessian fly was Asian in origin and had been known since at least 1768). When the British refused to accept imports of American wheat, Jefferson brought together a committee of the American Philosophical Society to investigate the fly. The members included Benjamin Rush, Caspar Wistar, Charles Thomson, and Benjamin Smith Barton. The committee produced a questionnaire for gathering information. When did the eruptions occur? On what part of the plant? Were other crops affected? Did manuring help? Were some varieties of wheat less susceptible than others? What effect did cold have? Did other animals eat the insect? And what farming practices affected it?[61] In other words, they wanted to learn the basic natural history of the insect and through that to find a control. It was a task for which Jefferson was ideally suited.

That year (1791), he and his great friend James Madison made a "northern journey" through New York and New England, one purpose of which was to see the problem in person. They started in New York State and proceeded to Lakes George and Champlain before returning through Vermont, down to Connecticut, and across to Long Island. The field trip was meant to be both informative and therapeutic; for both men it was billed as a welcome break from the pressures of politics. In part, however, it was also the sort of trip that politicians make today, reinforcing old alliances and making new friends. They covered some nine hundred miles in the month, always on the lookout for interesting and useful plants and trees, farming practices, and new inventions, both for home use and to develop exports. Jefferson was in his element. He was struck by the value of maple sugar as a substitute for imported sugar and later had some success in introducing the sugar maple tree at Monticello. As soon as he returned he ordered "Sugar maples. All you have." from the nurseryman William Prince.[62] At Lake George they were impressed by the dramatic landscape, the abundant fishes, and the "musketoes & gnats, & 2 kinds of biting flies." They looked at factories for processing barrels of fish, machines for drawing water from wells, and a nailery, where Jefferson took notes for his own nail workshop.

One of the last legs of the journey involved a trip across Long Island Sound from Connecticut. Before visiting the farm where the Hessian fly outbreak had first been noted, Jefferson indulged in yet another of his scientific preoccupations—Indian languages. He jotted down on the back of an envelope a vocabulary of some two hundred words from some women of the Algonkian Unquachog people.

From his interviews with farmers, Jefferson learned that the Hessian fly lays its eggs between the leaves and wheat stem of young plants. When the maggots hatch they feed by sucking the juices of the stem, stunting and weakening

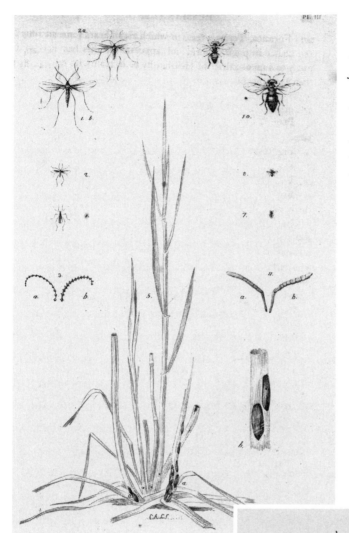

Life cycle of the Hessian fly, from Thomas Say, "Some Account of the Insect Known by the name of Hessian Fly," 1817 (Ewell Stewart Library, Academy of Natural Sciences)

Close-up view of Hessian fly, from Thomas Say, "Some Account of the Insect Known by the name of Hessian Fly" (Ewell Stewart Library, Academy of Natural Sciences) the plant, and causing it not to bear seeds. The maggots then become encased in a protective coating that resembles a flax seed, fall to the ground, and hatch out. The fly lives in the stubble until the new crop of wheat germinates, eggs are laid, and the cycle starts again. Of wheat varieties, a new bearded wheat produced a stronger stalk and was therefore less damaged by the insect. Later, Jefferson was sent batches of eggs to examine and he observed the life cycle under a primitive microscope.

Jefferson petitioned the British to the effect that the wheat grains themselves did not contain eggs or maggots and therefore could be safely imported. But to no avail. In fact, the whole affair petered out without resolution and the American Philosophical Society Committee did not make a formal report. There was no simple way to eradicate the fly. The natural history of the insect showed that the only way to reduce its ravages was to plant a variety called yellow bearded wheat, to burn the stubble fields after harvest, and to sow new seed as late as possible in the year. It also helped to manure the fields—this was always Jefferson's favorite remedy—so that the plants were as sturdy as possible. In other words, one had to practice good farming. The Hessian fly infestation continued. By 1797 it had crossed the Hudson and the Delaware, circled Chesapeake Bay, and attacked George Washington's wheat fields at Mount Vernon. It reached Monticello around 1811. The insect's numbers seemed to flourish erratically: there were good years and bad. Of his crop in 1817, Jefferson wrote we "must … be contented with so much … as that miserable insect will leave us. this remnant will scarcely feed us the present year, for such swarms of the Wheat-fly were never before seen in this country."[63] It is still a major pest. One of the more resistant varieties of modern bearded wheat is named for Jefferson.

• • •

By any account, Jefferson was a polymath—equally at home in mathematics, languages, architecture, philosophy, and science. Beyond the sheer range of his interests and learning, there is the remarkable fact of Jefferson's *capacity*. He was able to do so very many things, to follow so many interests, at once. While variously in Paris, Philadelphia, and New York in the service of his country, he could supervise the works at Monticello and monitor the economy of his plantations and the upbringing of his family, while still developing his many scientific interests. He wrote some twenty thousand letters. In all this, he found time not just for the observational kind of natural history but also its intellectual foundations.

One of the themes of natural history as it developed in the seventeenth and eighteenth century was a search for systems of classification. A classification system would not only arrange known animals or plants in a logical system, it would form a framework into which new discoveries could be slotted. The first part of the solution was to find a way of giving each species a unique name, so that it would not be confused with others (there are lots of "black birds," for example). It had been the genius of the Swedish botanist Linnaeus to create a system of double names—of which perhaps the most famous is that of our own species: *Homo sapiens*. From this he developed a hierarchical system: there are species other than *sapiens* in the genus *Homo* (the fossil *Homo neanderthalensis*, for example). There are more genera than *Homo* in the Family *Hominidae*, and more families than just the *Hominidae* in the order Primates. And so on. This might all sound dull and plodding stuff, but not to someone like Jefferson. He realized that systems like Linnaeus's represented nothing less than a common language that anyone in the world could understand.[64] He set a very modern example by using the new Linnaean system in his *Notes on the State of Virginia*.

Of course, not everyone shared Jefferson's view of the primacy of natural history, the values of the Linnaean system, or the disciplines of observation and data gathering. It would be fascinating to know his response to a letter he received from Thomas Mann Randolph, whom he had been advising on matters of education. Randolph told him: "I was long delighted with the charms of Natural History, but found at last that altho it was the most rational and agreeable amusement in which hours of relaxation could be employed, yet it was too trivial to spend a whole life in the prosecution of. Natural Philosophy appeared more deserving of a particular attention, the exalted nature of its subjects, and the utility which mankind in general derive from their investigation, seemed to offer a reward equal to the arduous undertaking. The sublime pleasure which the mind feels on the discovery of a Mathematical truth ...."[65]

Randolph went on to declare that he had resolved to study Politics!

Chapter Five

NOTES ON THE STATE OF VIRGINIA

For such a compulsive writer, it is surprising that Jefferson's only book was written almost by accident. Jefferson was an extraordinarily prolific correspondent, pouring out his thoughts and dreams, frustrations and triumphs, questions and answers, in some twenty thousand letters. But he only wrote one book of his own. Perhaps, having devoted several hours each day to correspondence, he had no time for anything more literary. When his term as governor of Virginia ended in 1781 and he was able to return to Monticello after British forces had sacked it—on their way to a resounding defeat at Yorktown—Jefferson had the opportunity to write his one book. The result is reckoned to be an American masterpiece. In *Notes on the State of Virginia*, among many other subjects, he revealed his extraordinary knowledge of natural history, and not just of his home state, but of all North America. It was also an exercise in patriotism. Jefferson did not intend to write this book, however. He came to the project in a roundabout way. In 1780, Francois Marquis de Barbé-Marbois, secretary to the French delegation in Philadelphia, was asked by his government to put together a report describing the new nation, from geography, geology, natural history, and agriculture to cities, harbors, politics, laws, and even the treatment of British royalist sympathizers after the war. If this had not been done quite openly, it might have been just the sort of thing that one could imagine a spy being asked to undertake. To gather information systematically (this was the age of the French Encyclopedists), Barbé-Marbois composed a list of twenty-two questions (see Appendix C) and copies of this questionnaire were sent or given to representatives of the thirteen new states.[66]

The list of questions for each state was the same, but the replies Barbé-Marbois received were wildly different. Perhaps not all of those who received the questionnaire replied. From South Carolina, New Jersey, and New Hampshire, the replies were brief—just a few pages. Barbé-Marbois's concerns were largely politi-

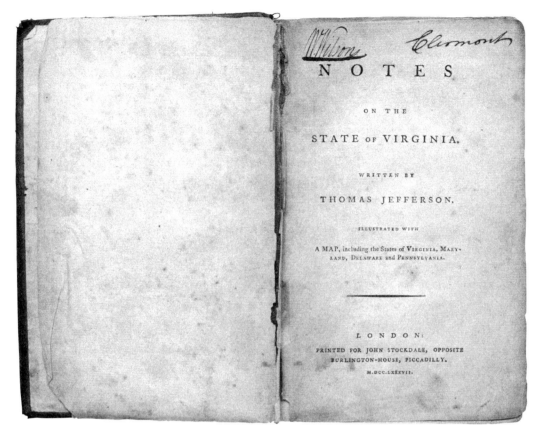

Title page of Notes on the State of Virginia *(Thomas Jefferson Foundation)*

cal, economic, and geographical; this is reflected in the reply of Thomas Bee concerning South Carolina. For natural history, Bee simply referred Barbé-Marbois to the account of North America by the English naturalist Mark Catesby.[67] The Rev. John Witherspoon of New Jersey did not mention natural history at all.[68] In contrast, the response of General John Sullivan for New Hampshire was distinctly assertive regarding the natural history of his homeland: "Perhaps few countries have Such a variety of animals for beside all kinds of European Animals moose Elks Deer Bears wolves Catermounts Foxes hares beaver rabbits otters minks Racoons Squirrels & other wild Quadrupeds are found in greater abundance here than in any other country—wild fowl are also found here in very great abundance our Seas Rivers & Lakes abound in Fish of almost Every sort."[69]

To learn about Virginia, Barbé-Marbois gave a copy of his questions to Joseph Jones, a member of that state's delegation in Philadelphia. But Jones evidently knew that Jefferson would want to speak for his homeland, so he sent it on to him. For Jefferson, this turned out to be a rare opportunity, a chance to pull together all his knowledge, contained in notes and records that he had, in his typically methodical way, been collecting for years, and write something informative for Barbé-Marbois, whom he had met in Philadelphia. They later came to know each other very well, and it was Barbé-Marbois who, as minister of the treasury for Napoleon I, negotiated for France the Louisiana Purchase of 1803 that so completely changed America's geography and destiny.

Barbé-Marbois did not know that Jefferson would be answering his questions and Jefferson was somewhat amused by this. "I am at present busily employed for Monsr. Marbois without his knowing it, and have to acknolege to him the mysterious obligation for making me much better acquainted with my own country than I ever was before."[70]

Had Barbé-Marbois known that Jefferson would be his informant, he would have been pleased to have a response from so great an expert, and perhaps just a little nervous about how long and argumentative that report might be. Jefferson, in fact, seized the opportunity to correct a number of misapprehensions, even downright libels, of North America that were current in France.

Jefferson set to work and sent off a reply to Barbé-Marbois in December 1781, explaining that his draft was incomplete and that he expected soon to be free to spend more time on the work; he meant that he would no longer be governor. Enforced rest due to a fall from his horse at Poplar Forest required him to sit still long enough to write, and he set to work in earnest, canvassing friends for information and sending them drafts to read. Jefferson's first plan for publication of the *Notes* had to be shelved when the costs seemed too high. Then, having been sent to Paris as minister, he had an edition of two hundred copies published there, and circulated them among his friends in May 1785. Threatened with pirated versions and translations, he allowed a new, revised version to be published in America in 1787.[71]

In the book-length version of *Notes*, Jefferson changed the order of Barbé-Marbois' questions and answers to something with a more logical development. It follows quite closely the plan of Robert Beverley's *The History and Present State of Virginia*, published in 1705.[72] He began with a section on the "exact ... limits and boundaries of the State of Virginia," and "A notice of its rivers ... and ... seaports." Next he gave a thorough description of the "mountains" in which he points out that they are part of a long series of ridges, running northeast to southwest, forming the northwestern boundary of the state. Here Jefferson ventured into an interpretation of the geological history that was quite at odds with his later views on the value of hypothetical geological constructions. He gave the "opinion that, in the valley where the Shenandoah and Potowmac (have cut) through the Blue ridge ... the mountains were formed first, that the rivers began to flow afterwards, that in this place particularly they have been dammed up by the Blue ridge of mountains and have formed an ocean which filled the whole valley; that, continuing to rise, they have at length broken over at this spot, and have torn the mountain down from its summit. The piles of rock .... (are) the evident marks of their disrupture and avulsion from their beds by the most powerful agents of nature." (In fact, this paragraph was submitted to Jefferson for *Notes* by Charles Thomson, secretary to Congress, with whom Jefferson exchanged a long series of letters, many on scientific matters.)

Along with "caverns," Jefferson described one of his favorite places in Virginia, the Natural Bridge near Lynchburg. He thought this was "the most sublime of Nature's works" and he loved the site so much that he bought it.[73] From geography, Jefferson proceeded to "Query XI: A notice of the mines, and other subterranean riches; trees, plants, fruits, &c." At first it might seem odd for Barbé-Marbois to have combined mines and minerals with animals and plants, all under one heading. But this was exactly a description of the subject that scholars, including Jefferson, included under the heading "Natural History;" their study was a matter of enumeration and description of nature. Mines and minerals were quickly disposed of, because Virginia is poorly endowed with ores of gold, silver, and copper, or with precious stones. Iron, coal, lead, and limestone were mined only in small quantities. Jefferson listed various useful "stones," including the niter from caves and salt at various salt springs or "licks," so called because they naturally attract wildlife and cattle. He mentioned various medicinal springs.

So far this was a quite conventional, if thorough, description of the attributes of Jefferson's home state. Passing on to "Vegetables" ("trees, plants, fruits, &c") one immediately feels that Jefferson's interest as an author has been more fully engaged. This is a subject he knew a lot about, as he demonstrated in detailed lists of plants under four headings: "1. Medicinal, 2. Esculent, 3. Ornamental, or 4. Useful for fabrication." Jefferson displayed his technical knowledge by listing both the common names and the scientific names in Latin according to the innovative new scheme of Linnaeus whose *Species Plantarum*, the work that revolutionized the whole study of nature, had been published only twenty years earlier. Typically, Jefferson did not attempt to list any of the plants, shrubs, or trees that fell outside his four categories, each of which is "useful." There was no list of wildflowers, for example, or of the kinds of plants that people planted in their flower beds; almost all the ornamentals he listed were trees.

Two notable items in Jefferson's lists are Jamestown Weed (jimson weed) and the pecan tree. Jefferson was fascinated by jimson weed because of its powerful, even lethal, narcotic and hallucinogenic properties. In a letter written on July 14 (Bastille Day) of 1813, he said that in the time of Robespierre, every Frenchman of "firmness" carried a preparation in his pocket "to anticipate the guillotine. It brings on the sleep of death as quietly as fatigue does the ordinary sleep, without the least struggle or motion."[74] The pecan tree had not been listed by European writers such as the great Linnaeus. In *Notes*, Jefferson was the first to describe it as a separate species from the white walnut or butternut. He gave a formal description in Latin in great professional style: "foliolis lanceolatis, acuminatis, serratis, tomentosis, fructu minore, ovato, compresso, vix insculpto, dulci, putamine, tenerrimo."[75]

Jefferson's lists of plants were essentially confined to species found in Virginia. When he turned to "animals," however, his scope widened to all of "America." The reason for this is that, as he expanded his responses to Barbé-Marbois into the full version of his *Notes*, Jefferson not only wanted to document the natural history of his beloved country, he had a particular, rather more political, mission in mind. This was another case where Jefferson could turn his knowledge of natural history into something useful—in this case a quasi-political weapon.

• • •

The greatest writer on natural history in the eighteenth century was Georges-Louis Leclerc, Comte de Buffon. His *Histoire Naturelle, Générale et Particulière* was published in forty-four quarto volumes between the years 1749 and 1809. In this huge work, Buffon and his collaborators covered the natural history of the whole world, as it was then known. It was the only such work and became the standard reference for scholars. But parts of the world were still extremely badly known. When it came to the Americas, Buffon's information was often incomplete or downright wrong, especially about North America. His book also contained an entirely false theory. Buffon claimed to have discovered nothing less than a fundamental principle concerning American wildlife; he called it his "degeneracy thesis." Jefferson summarized it as follows: "1. That the animals common both to the old and new world, are smaller in the latter. 2. That those peculiar to the new, are on a smaller scale. 3. That those that have been domesticated in both, have degenerated in America: and 4. That on the whole it [America] exhibits fewer species."[76] For Buffon, the principle extended beyond animals and plants to include the native peoples of the Americas as well.[77]

Buffon was not the first European writer to malign the Americas. He had never visited the New World, and his remarks were a mixture of other people's firsthand observations and secondhand opinions. Don Antonio d'Ulloa (*Relación histórica del viaje hecho de orden de su Majestad a la América Meridional*, 1748) was a Spanish naval officer who traveled in South America, and the idea of American degeneracy appears in his writings. Two influential French writers to elaborate the theory later were the Abbé Raynal (*Histoire Philosophique et Politique*, 1770) and the Abbé Corneille de Pauw (*Récherches Philosophiques sur les Americains*, 1768). Raynal had never been to America or seen an Indian, although de Pauw and Ulloa had. Jefferson said of de Pauw that "he seems to have read the writings of travelers only to collect and republish their lies. It is really remarkeable that in three volumes 12mo. of small print it is scarcely possible to find one truth...."[78]

Strong support for the theory of degeneracy, in Buffon's view, came from the supposed fact that domestic animals, when transplanted from Europe to the Americas, were always weaker. One of the early authors to indicate the poor growth of European cattle in America had been the Swedish-Finnish scholar Peter Kalm, a man whose work Jefferson otherwise admired. During his trip to Philadelphia in September 1748, Kalm noted that "the cattle degenerate by degrees here, and become smaller."[79] He thought the cause was the climate. On the other hand, William Byrd, eleven years earlier, had offered what may be at least a partial explanation: "in Virginia ... the grass is extremely beautiful and good (and) the winters very short. Therefore very little hay (is) needed ... cattle wander in the runs all winter long ... because of this ... they grow very thin, and remain small, which does not happen if they are given hay, and kept in stables."[80] (Byrd also promised that Virginia was such a wonderful place that even sick people going there would soon be healthy; but "who ever desires to die soon, just go to Carolina.")

The only place where the Americas could be granted any kind of superiority by d'Ulloa, Buffon, and their followers, was in having more numerous poisonous snakes and insects than Europe—a superiority that was, itself, an inferiority! De Pauw wrote particularly dramatically on this subject: "(in Surinam) caterpillars, butterflies, centipedes, scarabs, spiders, frogs and toads were found in gigantic size for their species, and multiplied beyond imagining ... Even today, the oldest European colonies in America are not yet cleansed of filthy or poisonous animals whose propagation is encouraged by the atmosphere."[81]

All this seemed rather typical of European arrogance and ignorance where America was concerned. A particular weakness of the arguments was that Buffon and his informants tended to lump together the whole of North, South, and Central America as one "America," leading inevitably to wildly aberrant generalizations. The origins of the degeneracy theory, and the motives behind it, were complicated. While Buffon's errors may have been simply inadvertent and were posed in a scientific context, he did not hesitate to build strongly on the ideas of d'Ulloa. The latter's views, like those of Raynal and de Pauw, were as much political rhetoric as scientific discourse. A popular line, taken by d'Ulloa and Raynal, was to see North and South America as both physically and morally unhealthy places. Their cultures had begun with deported criminals and were based on colonialism, exploitation of natural resources, extermination or subjugation of the native peoples, and slavery. De Pauw asked, "Would any physicist of Antiquity ever have suspected that this same planet had two hemispheres so different from the other one of which would be conquered, subjugated and devoured by the other just as soon as it was discovered?"[82]

Another factor was that, whereas in France, and in Europe generally, the intelligentsia were mostly aristocratic, North America was seen as a dangerously anti-aristocratic place. Above all, there was the growing realization that the New World, and particularly the new nation emerging out of the thirteen former British colonies, was not inferior at all; it might in fact be *superior*. The confident North Americans or Federo-Americans (to use a term of Jefferson's that never caught on) were not reticent about boasting of the boundless lands and natural resources of their new world and were proud of the opportunities it presented. Nor were they reticent about the fact that, even under a colonial regime, they had created a welcome home for the disaffected of Europe. From Boston to Virginia a new landed class was emerging. The cities were growing rapidly; Philadelphia was one of the largest cities in the British Empire. Most importantly, the Federo-Americans were creating a dangerous new kind of democracy, one that could be threatening to the European oligarchy if it caught on, and therefore needed to be maligned.[83]

Indeed, not everyone agreed with the opinion of the New World for which Buffon became the cheerleader, especially if they had traveled there. The Marquis de Chastellux, who had been third in command of the French forces at the Battle of Yorktown, spent three years traveling in the country and became a particular friend of Jefferson. He not only praised the beauties and plentitude of the American lands, he was impressed by the growing sophistication of the cities. Meanwhile, as the precarious financial security of the fledgling United States depended heavily on loans from Europe, anything detrimental to the new country had to be countered.

Of course, Buffon was right in some respects: there were many genuine and significant differences between the animals and plants of the Old World and the New. Buffon speculated as to their causes in terms of history. Where did they come from? Recent discoveries by Russian explorers suggested that there was a route by which animals could have passed overland between Kamchatka and America, via the islands of the Bering Straits. On its eastern side, North America was separated by ocean from Europe and Asia. That would suggest an affinity of the animals of North America to those of far eastern Siberia. On the other had, Buffon thought that the mammals of North America "have a stronger resemblance to the quadrupeds of the north of Europe. It is the same with the animals which belong to the temperate climates."[84] In either case, having arrived in America, they had degenerated.

These questions could be repeated when one considered the native peoples. Just as European scholars could not decide where the flora and fauna of the New World had originated, so they also wondered how to categorize the "Indians" of the North and South. They apparently lacked literacy and civilization, which was a strange claim to make of the Inca and Aztec cultures of South America. Were they merely the kind of primitives who lived in the state of grace that Rousseau thought preceded the acquisition of the refinements of civilization? Or were they degenerated versions of other, older races that had migrated from somewhere else? If so, where had these peoples come from? One idea popular with many Europeans, including the first settlers in Massachusetts, was that the Indians represented the remnants of one of the lost tribes of Israel![85]

Buffon had an innate distaste for Rousseau's concept of "noble savages" and developed a scientific explanation for American degeneracy in terms of climate. His basic claim, again seized upon and amplified by Raynal and de Pauw, was that, unlike Europe, America was always cold, wet, and unhealthy. Further, this affected the quality of food. Finally, and most interestingly, he suggested there was everywhere a feedback between the progress of civilization and climate: where there were more people and a well-developed agriculture, the climate improved. As there were far fewer people in the New World, he argued, they had had a smaller effect on the environment, and thus had improved the climate less.

Much of Buffon's information had come from reports of French travelers and traders who had visited arctic or subarctic Canada. They would certainly attest that it was cold there. From this, de Pauw wildly over-generalized, claiming for instance that anywhere in America, if you dug down six or seven inches, the soil would be icy cold. In fact, much of the rest of North America was really hotter than Europe and perhaps drier, although Buffon had been perfectly correct in stating that, if one looked at places on the same latitude, the comparison was unfavorable to the New World. Notable examples would be Quebec and Paris, Boston and Seville, or Hudson Bay and Edinburgh. Buffon thought that this was because east winds blew onto America from across a cold ocean. On the other hand, any traveler to Philadelphia (let alone Virginia) during the summer would hardly have thought the climate there cool. As for the vast tropical realms, they were obviously hot and often wet.

Another suggestion of Buffon was that perhaps "America" really was a new world—in the literal, geological, sense. "We are inclined to believe that [the New World] is actually more recent, and has continued longer than the rest of the globe under the waters of the ocean."[86] It therefore had had less time to mature. Another possibility was that the Great Flood of Noah had reached the Americas later, and had therefore only receded more recently. This would help account for the terrible cold and wet climate. Basically, whatever the cause, the Americas formed an awful place in which the climate had always been inhospitable to animals, plants, and people.

Buffon's "great theory" remained a hot topic of conversation for decades. It must, however, have been hard to maintain a theory of physical and intellectual inferiority in the American people when two such intellectual giants as Jefferson and Franklin were living in Paris. And they were not merely intellectual giants. Franklin, as reported by Abbé Bonnet, famously refuted Buffon's thesis at a dinner party he hosted, at which Raynal was a guest. Taking advantage of the chance of who had been invited, he asked all the Americans present to stand and then all the French. The Americans were all far taller. (This general disparity, which held until very recent times, is no longer true; now Europeans are on average taller than Americans.) Raynal himself was a "shrimp," but Franklin gracefully turned the tables against himself by pointing out that he was quite short himself.

In France, admiration for America grew after the Revolution and the creation of the United States and then France's own Revolution. Raynal came to see America, not Britain or France, as the leader in promoting liberty and democracy. But that was in 1780 and a bit too late for Jefferson. However, adding to the insult of the French works, the theory of degeneracy remained extremely popular long after their authors had retracted or diluted their claims. Scandalous as these notions were to Americans, Europeans loved them. In Britain, even while (and perhaps because) thousands of people cheerfully departed for this supposed hell on earth, the popularity of the "degeneracy" theory continued unabated. William Robertson, a Scot and another expert who never set foot in the Americas, wrote a four-volume *History of America* (1777), in which he repeated the statements about the Indians. It went into many editions in England and there was even an American edition in 1812. An equally popular work in Europe was Oliver Goldsmith's treatise *A History of the Earth, and Animated Nature* (1774)—a sort of English language version of Buffon. There he repeated the claims of the French and added others that Buffon had omitted. So something had to be done.

• • •

No doubt General Sullivan of New Hampshire also had Buffon in mind when he insisted on the supremacy of the animals in his state, in his own response to Barbé-Marbois' questions. Jefferson was not so restrained. Unlike most of the European writers, Jefferson had a wealth of firsthand information about North American natural history, accumulated over many years. He also wrote to friends asking for data and for specimens and especially sought information about the biggest possible specimens. Jefferson then took Buffon's arguments apart, piece by piece, and refuted them. He did not try to speak for, or about, Central or South

America; but his *Notes on the State of Virginia* were, in many places, notes on North America.

To claim that the supposed degeneracy of life was due to the climate in "America" being cooler and more humid was an extraordinary charge to apply to the whole of two continents, with Central America and the Caribbean Islands in between. And in any case, Jefferson stated, Buffon's information about climate was simply wrong. North America was not colder and wetter on average than Europe. And, in countering Buffon on factual grounds, Jefferson was able to use his own writings against him. Buffon had actually written that, in Europe, the cold, moist countries were the most favorable for the growth of cattle. It was also the case that heat and moisture were conducive to the growth of plants and, since plants are the food of the animals, to animals as well. There was no geological evidence on which to base a claim about the relative ages of continents.

Rather than continuing to argue abstractions, Jefferson proposed a simple empirical test: a direct comparison of the sizes of mammals in Europe and America. In *Histoire Naturelle*, Buffon had made an analysis of three categories of mammals. If the same species occurred in both continents, Buffon said they were smaller in America; mammals that were found only in America were also smaller than anything in Europe; and European animals that had been domesticated in America were always smaller than in the homeland. But Buffon's data was anecdotal. In contradiction, Jefferson presented real numbers, in three corresponding tables. Naturally enough the results turned out to be very much in America's favor. In Jefferson's tables, the American black bear was three times heavier than the European bear, whereas Buffon had claimed they were "smaller and darker." The beaver in America was twice as heavy, as were the otter and flying squirrel. His data comparing the European red deer with the Virginia deer showed parity. There were some odd omissions in the tables. He did not have weights for the wolf or red fox in America. Getting weights for the polar bear (white bear) was presumably difficult. Some of his comparisons were dubious because in fact different species were involved.

All together, Jefferson's comparisons showed the American versions of common species as bigger. "Of 26 quadrupeds common to both countries, 7 are said to be larger in America, 7 of equal size, and 12 not sufficiently examined ... (That) impeaches the first member of the assertion, that of the animals common to both countries, the American are smallest." As for species that are only found either in Europe or in America, Jefferson was happy to cite the American elk and cougar as being bigger than any relative in Europe. More importantly, in his lists Jefferson counted seventy-four mammal species, from tapir to ground squirrel (chipmunk) that are native to the Americas, while only eighteen could be counted as native to Europe. "The first of these 74 (it was the tapir) weighs more than the whole column of Europeans." Buffon, on the other hand, when he extended his lists to Africa, could count the elephant, rhinoceros, hippopotamus, and many other very large species and show that there was nothing of comparable size anywhere in the Americas. Buffon had actually mocked the fact that the tapir was the largest mammal that Americans could point to. He could also make much of the fact that there were no large mammals at all in Central America. Buffon did, however, record that there had, in former times, been large mammals in South America of which only fossils are now found. That fact supported his idea that the modern faunas were degenerate.[87]

Jefferson was a lawyer, and it is not to denigrate that profession, but merely to note a set of rhetorical styles and stratagems, to report that Jefferson did not mind shading the truth in making his points against Buffon. For domestic animals, Jefferson only had data for the cow—listed at a most unlikely maximum of 763 pounds in Europe and 2,500 in America. He had no good numbers for horse, ass, hog, or sheep in Europe; but he presented some anecdotal evidence of the hardiness of American breeds. "I have seen a hog weigh 1050 lb after the blood, bowels, and hair had been taken from him ... yet this hog was probably not within fifty generations of the European stock." Jefferson was careful wherever possible to support his data with quotations from European zoologists like d'Aubenton, Mark Catesby, and Peter Kalm. He stated that Kalm was "the best informed of any naturalist who has ever written," and this was surely a dig at Buffon, who would expect to claim that title. In fact, throughout this section of *Notes*, Jefferson proceeded by sometimes taking the high road (presenting unassailable facts) and sometimes resorting to barbs. For example, he said, "It does not appear that Messr. De Buffon, and d'Aubenton have measured, weighed, or seen" American animals. And he repeated, in his best poker-faced style, Buffon's own statement to the effect that he loved best someone who corrected him in an error, because an error corrected became a fact. In this case, "one sentence of his [Buffon's] book must do him immortal honour." Under the veneer of politeness, it was all quite nasty.

Aside from a number of comparisons of sizes (which, in retrospect, seem quite debatable on both sides), Buffon thought that in the elephant he had incontrovertible evidence of the superior size of Old World animals. Jefferson, however, was holding three aces. Nothing in Europe was as big as the American elk or the American moose (also known by its French name of orignal) and, looming above all, Jefferson had the example of the elephant relative that we know as the mastodon (Chapter Five). The mastodon was more than one and one-half times taller and longer than either the mammoth that had once lived in both Europe and North America or the living African and Asiatic elephants. Jefferson baldly included the mastodon in his enumeration of living North American wildlife because he believed that members of the species were still extant in the great unexplored western wilderness. On the other hand, Jefferson wisely did not bring up the subject of the fossil "Irish elk" (actually a giant deer found across Europe). It was inconveniently large, but all European zoologists agreed that it was undeniably extinct. Jefferson did not believe that any animals became extinct, but he was evidently happy to let that one pass.

After the mastodon, nothing suited Jefferson's argument better than the moose. The moose, with its magnificent antlers, was well known to European travelers, especially French-Canadians, although they tended to confuse it with the elk. It was a species that thrived in the cold and wet—just the conditions under which, according to Buffon, it should be stunted and degenerate. Live moose had even been imported to Europe from time to time (and, ironically, they had not thrived). In England, the Marquis of Rockingham had one in 1770; King George III was presented with a specimen in the early 1770s; the Duke of Richmond acquired specimens in 1770 and 1773. One of them was drawn for an illustration in a Dutch edition of Buffon's *Natural History*, and its portrait was also drawn by George Stubbs, perhaps the greatest painter of horses of all time.[88] All of these specimens, however, were relatively juvenile and/or female and had suffered a long, difficult sea voyage. None survived long in England.

Mastodon lower jaw (Thomas Jefferson Foundation)

When he arrived in Paris in 1785, Jefferson sent Buffon a copy of *Notes* and the skin of a large panther (which Buffon had confused with the cougar). Buffon invited him to dinner at the Jardin du Roi and admitted the mistake over the panther. But he was not going to give up his main point without a struggle, refusing to believe, without actually seeing specimens, that American deer were as large as European (actually the Virginia deer is not as large as the European red deer) or that the moose was so much larger than the reindeer that, as Jefferson is reputed to have told him, the reindeer could walk under the belly of the American moose (it could not). "In my conversations with the Count de Buffon ... I find him absolutely unacquainted with our Elk and our deer. He has hitherto beleived that our deer never had horns more than a foot long...."[89]

So Jefferson wrote from Paris to his friend General John Sullivan in New Hampshire asking him to obtain specimens of the moose, caribou, and elk. He specified that the bones of the head and legs and the hooves should be left in the skin so that they could easily be mounted in a lifelike manner. Trophy-sized moose were not so common in New England that Sullivan could lay his hands on one easily. But eventually, after some trials and tribulations, a party of twenty men ventured into Vermont and shot a good specimen at least seven feet tall. Sullivan sent a whole box of specimens of large mammals to Paris—along with a hefty bill. They arrived, Jefferson reported, "all in good enough condition except that a good deal of

The Duke of Richmond's Second Bull Moose, *George Stubbs, 1773 (Special Collections Department, Glasgow University Library)*

the hair of the Moose had fallen off.... I am in hopes Monsieur de Buffon will be able to have him stuffed and placed on his legs in the king's cabinet...."[90] (In fact the antlers that Sullivan sent were small and belonged to a different individual.)

Accounts of what happened next differ. Some think that Jefferson set up the moose skeleton at his apartments and invited Buffon to visit.[91] In fact, Jefferson sent the box of specimens (doubtless not smelling particularly sweet) straight to the Jardin du Roi. In a long letter to Buffon, Jefferson wrote: "I am happy to be able to present to you at this moment the bones and skin of a Moose, the horns of [another] individual of the same species, the horns of the Caribou, the el[k,] the deer, the spiked horned buck, and the Roebuck of America."[92] He pointed out that "the Moose, the Round horned elk, and the American deer are species not existing in Europe." He tried to present his facts gracefully, so as not to give offense. "I wish these spoils, Sir, may have the merit of adding any thing new to the treasures of nature which so fortunately come under your observation.... They will in that case be some gratification to you...."[93]

As the elderly Buffon was away when the specimens arrived, they were entrusted to his associate, L. J. M. d'Aubenton. This is confirmed in a letter that Jefferson

Moose antlers, circa 1784–1786 (Thomas Jefferson Foundation)

wrote to General Sullivan, reporting on the fate of his specimens; "he [Buffon] was in the country when I sent the box to the Cabinet, so that I have as yet no answer from him."[94] Daniel Webster, who visited Jefferson years later, was the source of a different version of the story. In his recollection, Jefferson invited Buffon to his house and, when Buffon saw the skins and skeletons, he "immediately acknowledged his error. 'I should have consulted you, Monsieur,'" he is supposed to have said, "before I published my book on natural history, and then I should have been sure of my facts."[95] As the specimens had already been sent to the museum, this cannot be a correct account. Jefferson did later claim that Buffon had given up his position and had promised to say so in his next volume, but that Buffon died before he could do so.[96] It would be nice to think that Buffon acquiesced so gracefully to Jefferson, but there is no hard evidence that he did.

• • •

It was an interesting reflection on the state of American natural science that, when Jefferson made a list of American birds for *Notes on the State of Virginia*, he principally had to rely on the lists in Catesby's book. He also added another twelve species from his own knowledge and those of his friends. He apparently was not aware of the lists in William Byrd's essay on the natural history of Virginia (published in German in 1737) in which most of the birds are mentioned and described.

Jefferson's list of eighty-eight species shows that almost all of the common birds of eastern North America had by then been identified.

In their theories of American degeneracy, the French had not been content with maligning American wild and domestic mammals. American birds were also thought to be inferior to their European counterparts and particularly in the matter of song. In Europe, the most beautiful bird song is always reckoned to be that of the nightingale, which happens to be inconspicuous and a drab, brown thing. Sadly reduced in numbers today, it is eagerly listened for in the six-week period in spring when it sets up its woodland territory. The European song thrush also has a lovely song and for a much longer season. In compensation for lacking beautiful voices, American birds (especially in the tropical realms) were reckoned to have magnificent plumage. That might have been true of the birds of the American tropics, but it was not true of America's best songster, and one of Jefferson's favorite birds, the mockingbird (or mock bird). The mockingbird, like the nightingale, is a somewhat drab creature but it not only has a superb repertoire of melodious songs, it is an adept mimic of other birds. Jefferson loved the mockingbird so much that he kept one in a cage at Monticello and tamed it so that it would perch on his shoulder and take food from his mouth.

The supposed poverty of American bird life was not something that Buffon invented. As usual, French zoologists had been badly informed by early travelers who brought back to Europe only miserable dried skins, which did little to represent the full glory of bird life across the Atlantic.[97] Jefferson did not address the issue of song, but his friend and political ally Alexander Wilson, author of *American Ornithology* (1808–1814) did. Wilson pointed out that, for example, two influential naturalists, Mark Catesby and John Edwards, had mistakenly assumed that the European song thrush (lovely song) was the same species as (and had degenerated into) the American wood thrush (poor song). Refuting all this was going to be a long and tedious business, especially when other authors, like the popular Oliver Goldsmith (*Animated Nature*, 1774), repeated Buffon's claims without pausing to question them.

Buffon did not go quite so far as to claim that his principle of degeneracy applied to the white population when they crossed the Atlantic, although de Pauw and Raynal certainly did. Buffon left that inference to his readers without spelling it out, but he did rather unsubtly state that the New World had produced no poets or other intellectuals. Jefferson again had a ready, and angry, answer: "When we shall have existed as a people as long as the Greeks did before they produced a Homer, the Romans a Virgil, the French a Racine and Voltaire, the English a Shakespeare and Milton, should this reproach be still true, we will enquire from what unfriendly causes it has proceeded … but … In war we have produced a Washington … In physics we have produced a Franklin, than whom no one of the present age has made more important discoveries … We have supposed Mr. Rittenhouse second to no astronomer living…." He went on to add a dig at the British: "The sun of her glory is fast descending to the horizon. Her philosophy has crossed the Channel, her freedom the Atlantic, and herself seems passing to … awful dissolution…."[98]

In summarizing all the evidence against Buffon's ideas about American animal life, Jefferson wrote a rather outrageous paragraph in which he offset his barbs with silky flattery: "I only mean to suggest a doubt, whether the bulk and faculties of animals depend on the side of the Atlantic on which their food happens to grow, or which furnishes the elements of which they are compounded? Whether nature has enlisted herself as a Cis or Trans-Atlantic partisan? I am induced to suspect, there has been more eloquence than sound reasoning displayed in support of this theory; that it is one of those cases where judgment has been seduced by a glowing pen: and whilst I render every tribute of honour and esteem to the celebrated Zoologist, who has added, and is still adding, so many precious things to the treasures of science, I must doubt whether in this instance he has not cherished error also, by lending her for a moment his vivid imagination and bewitching language."[99] The whole affair, for Jefferson, was another example of the "poetry of eloquence, and the uncertainties of theories."

Chapter Six

The Mastodon and the Great-claw

Thomas Jefferson has sometimes been called the father of vertebrate paleontology, the field of study that has today burgeoned to cover an extraordinary range of animals including dinosaurs, mammals, birds, reptiles, amphibians, fish, and, of course, our human and pre-human ancestors. And it is true that he made some observations on fossil mammals at a crucial time in the development of American science. Fossils were familiar to Jefferson; not only had he read about them, he had collected fossil shells from Virginia. Jefferson was not one of those who doubted, as did many of the time, that fossils were the remains of once-living animals preserved in the rock and as rock.[100] But fossils had, for centuries, presented natural scientists with a number of problems. If they were the remains of real animals, how were they formed, and how did the remains of seashells, the most commonly found fossils, come to be enclosed in rocks high up in mountains? Was it true, as many fossils seemed to indicate, that the world had in past times been populated with animals and plants that no longer exist? The idea that fossils represented the remains of creatures that are now extinct went against everything that was conventionally believed about the literal truth of the Book of Genesis. Nowhere in the Bible did it say that there had been multiple events of Creation, or that God had somehow made mistakes that he later corrected.

Not only did Jefferson know about fossil shells, which could be found in many places along the eastern seaboard when he came to write his *Notes*, he knew a very special kind of fossil—one that would eventually help fix for once and for all and totally against his own philosophical leanings—that extinction of animals and plants was a real phenomenon of nature and that the earth was much older than the Bible said. The fossils in question were remains of a huge relative of the elephants. They were first discovered by farmers at the beginning of the eighteenth century along the Hudson River in New York State. The Reverend Cotton

Mather learned of them and sent a description to a friend at the Royal Society in London.[101] The next find was made by a French military officer in 1737 at a spot just south of the Ohio River and present-day Cincinnati. The place was appropriately named the Big Bone Lick, and large numbers of fossil bones and teeth, together with tusks, were entombed there in an ancient marsh. The place was fed by a salt spring to which animals had evidently migrated for millennia and then become trapped in the mud and died. The most commonly found remains were of teeth, naturally enough as they are the densest part of the skeleton and least susceptible to decay. Each great tooth weighed two to four pounds. There were also thigh bones more than four feet long, and tusks measuring some fifteen feet or more. For example, James Kenny, a trader at Fort Pitt in 1762 reported "Robert Pusey … come here from ye Shawanna Town, being a Prissoner there about 5 years; he brought a Tooth weigh'd 4 ½ lb & say these teeth are Esteemed, that there are Horns about 12 foot long, as I suppose is ye Eye teeth of Elephants … none of ye Indians can remember of seeing any of these Creatures alive, neither do they Know who kill'd them."[102]

Early diaries suggest that these fossils were known from many places. Kenny wrote of a story of a creature living beyond the Mississippi, the "Rhinosses or Elephant Master, being a very large Creature of a Dark Colour having a long Strong horn growing upon his nose (wth which he kills Elephants) a Short tail like an Elk; two of sd horns he seen fixd over a Gate at St Augustine, & that its ye bnes of Some of these lies down in Buffelo lick by ye Ohio, wher ye Great teeth Comes from."[103] Because of the tusks, the remains obviously resembled those of an elephant. Furthermore, Peter Kalm, in July 1749, was told of a skeleton seen in the "country of the Illinois" where there was a skeleton "of prodigious bulk, and had white teeth, about ten inches long. It was looked upon as the skeleton of an elephant … the figure of the whole snout was yet to be seen, though it was half mouldered away."[104] The teeth were anomalous, however. Instead of having low parallel ridges on their surfaces for grinding plant food, as did the teeth of other kinds of elephants, these had a number of big cone-shaped cusps. It was these cusps, with their resemblance to the dugs on a sow or bitch, that eventually gave the animal its modern name—mastodon (breast-tooth). These teeth set off a huge debate among scholars of the time. Were they the teeth of an herbivore like the modern elephant, or some kind of strange (and dangerous) flesh-eater? The mysterious beast was often referred to as the "incognitum" (unknown).

A kind of an herbivorous fossil elephant—the mammoth—had long been known to travelers to Siberia. There, the remains were preserved in frozen soils and mud. Perhaps the American incognitum was a variety of that animal. Benjamin Franklin summed up the debate about the teeth in a letter to a French friend who was an expert on the Siberian mammoth: "Some of Our naturalists here … contend that these are not the Grinders of Elephants but of some carnivorous Animal unknown, because such Knobs or Prominences on the Face of the Tooth are not to be found on those of Elephants, and only, as they say, on those of carnivorous Animals. But it appears to me that Animals capable of carrying such large heavy Tusks, must themselves be large Creatures, too bulky to have the Activity necessary for pursuing and taking Prey, and therefore I am inclin'd to think those Knobs only a small Variety. Animals of the same kind and Name often differing more materially, and that those Knobs might be useful to grind the small Branches of Trees, as to chaw Flesh. However, I should be glad to have your opinion, and to know from you whether any of the kind have been found in Siberia."[105]

Various teeth and bones of the mastodon found their way from the "Ohio Country" via traders to London (where Franklin saw them) and Paris. In 1783, a Dr. John Morgan had assembled a collection of them in Philadelphia, and there Jefferson saw them. One of those teeth was beautifully drawn by Charles Willson Peale. What was the "incognitum"? The consensus was that it ought to have been some kind of mammoth, and therefore a relative of the elephants, except for the problem of the teeth. Two views then developed. One group of scholars thought that it was simply a deviant mammoth; another thought that the bones and tusks were remains of the mammoth, but that they had become mixed up with the teeth of a hippopotamus. The first person to propose this theory was Buffon's associate d'Aubenton in Paris. If the mastodon was simply a kind of mammoth, it was a vegetarian; if the teeth were those of a flesh-eating carnivore, then it truly was an

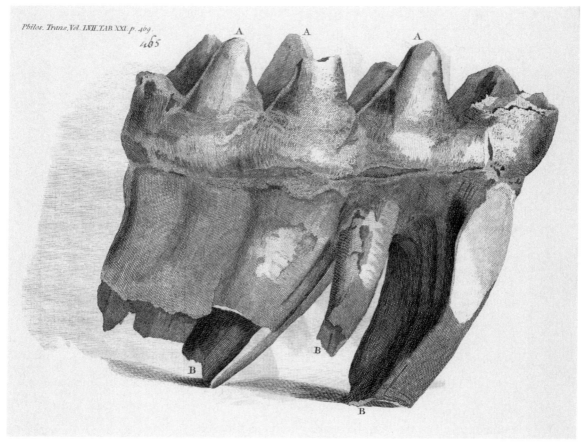

Mastodon tooth from Peter Collinson, "An Account of Some Very Large Fossil Teeth Found in North America," 1767 (Ewell Stewart Library, Academy of Natural Sciences)

incognitum of some other, more exciting sort. (Never mind that hippos are also herbivorous!)

This was a situation tailor-made for Jefferson's keen eye and rational mind. For him, the mastodon was not merely interesting in the scientific sense, it was also immensely useful politically.[106] In 1782, George Rogers Clark went to Big Bone Lick and got some specimens. They confirmed that the mastodon was huge and might have been a ferocious, carnivorous predator. It was the perfect answer to Buffon's sneers about the supposed inferiority of American fauna and flora. Not only could Jefferson show a moose to the French, he could call upon the mastodon (which Jefferson usually referred to, confusingly, as a mammoth). In fact, in his section on animals for *Notes on the State of Virginia*, he led off with the mastodon.[107] Jefferson felt secure in including the mastodon in his list of the (superior) American fauna in *Notes* because he genuinely believed it was still alive, "why should I omit it, as if it did not exist?" He was happy to state that "the bones of the mammoth which have been found in America, are as large as those found in the old world." [108] The "mammoth" was particularly useful in the debate with Buffon because the latter already knew of its existence and its size. "The skeleton of the mammoth (for so the incognitum has been called) bespeaks an animal of five or six times the cubic volume of an elephant, as Mons. de Buffon has admitted …" with grinders "five times as large … the grinding surface studded with four or five rows of blunt points…." [109]

This was the biggest American mammal and perfectly suited to defending America's honor—except in two respects. Things would have been so much more satisfactory if it had still been alive and if it actually was a carnivore. Jefferson would have preferred it to be so, but his head told him to be cautious; so he compromised by repeating an Indian myth about the existence of mastodons in the West, and merely stated that it was the "tradition of the Indians" to think it was a flesh eater. A Philadelphian naturalist, Judge George Turner, had fewer compunctions than Jefferson about claims for the ferocity and athleticism of the mastodon. He went to Big Bone Lick and collected his own materials in 1798. His view of the mastodon was just what was needed for a symbol of American power and superiority. "May it not be inferred, that as the largest and swiftest quadrupeds were appointed for his food, he necessarily was endowed with great strength and activity?—that, as the immense volume of the creature would unfit him for coursing after his prey through thickets and woods, Nature had furnished him with the power of taking it by a mighty leap?—That this power of springing to a great distance was requisite to the more effectual concealment of his bulky volume while lying in wait for prey? The Author of existence is wise and just in all his works. He never confers an appetite without the power to gratify it. With the agility and ferocity of the tiger; with a body of unequalled magnitude and strength, it is possible the Mammoth may have been at once the terror of the forest and of man! And may not the human race have made the extirpation of this terrific disturber a common cause?"[110]

One reason that so many people could entertain such wild notions about the mastodon was that very few in America had ever seen a live elephant. They drew their meager information from books and pictures. The first live elephant was brought to America in 1796 by Captain Jacob Crowninshield. This Indian elephant's name was Buffon![111] Equally ironically, many more slaves than whites had seen an elephant and there are several instances of slaves recognizing that mastodon teeth dug out of the earth had belonged to an elephant. In North Carolina, Mark Catesby reported, there "was dug out of the Earth three or four teeth of a large animal, which, by the concurring Opinion of all the Negroes, native Africans, that saw them, were grinders of an Elephant."[112]

In the same withering prose with which he demolished Buffon's arguments about the degeneracy of the American fauna, Jefferson took on the suggestion that the teeth were those of a hippo. The "tusks and skeletons are much larger than those of the elephant, and the grinders [teeth] many times greater than those of the hippopotamus, and essentially different in form.... It will not be said that the hippopotamus and elephant came always to the same spot, the former to deposit his grinders, and the latter his tusks and skeleton. For what became of the parts not deposited there? We must agree then that these remains belong to each other...."[113]

There remained two interesting questions abut the mastodon, however. If it was a kind of elephant, what was it doing in Ohio (now northern Kentucky), where the winters are long and cold? The same could be asked about the mammoths in Siberia. And were any mastodons still alive? It was Franklin who most sagaciously addressed the question of climate. His conclusion was that either the mastodon was an animal adapted for colder climates, as the Siberian mammoth must have been, or that carcasses of the beast had somehow been transported many hundreds of miles: something Noah's Flood could not have achieved. Another, more intriguing, possibility was that the climate of the earth had changed. As Jefferson put it, either an internal fire had made the earth much warmer in ancient times, or perhaps the obliquity of the ecliptic had changed "so ... as to include within the tropics all those regions in which the bones are found; the tropics being … the natural limits of habitation for the elephant."[114]

Jefferson's final opinion was that the mastodon was an animal "resembling the elephant in his tusks, and general anatomy, while his nature was in other respects extremely different." In other words, it was a relative of living elephants (African and Indian) that was adapted for living in a colder climate. Nature seemed to Jefferson to have drawn "a belt of separation between these two tremendous animals" and around the globe had assigned the elephant to the south of a zone between about 30 and 36 degrees north latitude, and the incognitum to the north.[115] As for extinction, Jefferson was philosophically opposed to the whole concept. "Such is the oeconomy of nature, that no instance can be produced of her having permitted any one race of her animals to become extinct; of her having formed any link in her great work so weak as to be broken."[116]

• • •

While many in Philadelphia's scientific elite remained excited about the mastodon and the debates over its identity, habits, and possible extinction, most realized that more material was needed. As the Rev. Nicholas Collin, a keen natural scientist, said: "The vast Mammot, is perhaps yet stalking through the western wilderness; but if he is no more, let us carefully gather his remains, and even try to find a whole skeleton of this giant, to whom the elephant was but a calf."[117] Jefferson remained convinced of the possible existence of the mastodon and other monsters beyond the Mississippi, and he may have been encouraged by the persistent rumors brought back by travelers and frontier dwellers. In 1797 he chaired a committee at the American Philosophical Society charged with finding "one or more entire skeletons of the Mammoth, so called, and of such other unknown animals as either have been, or hereafter may be discovered in America …the committee suggest to Gentlemen who may be in the way of inquiries of that kind, that the Great Bone Lick on the Ohio, and other places where there may be mineral salt, as the most eligible spots." Reflecting Jefferson's broad interests, the committee was also asked to investigate the remains of "ancient Fortifications, Tumuli, and other Indian works of art."[118] All this eventually led to the commissioning of the Lewis and Clark expedition of 1804 to 1806. Not everyone shared Jefferson's zeal for mastodons, however, and the topic became quite politicized. John Adams wrote: "The Spirit of Political Party has seized upon the Bones of this huge animal, because the head of a Party has written something about them, and has made them a subject of more conversation and Investigation than they merit."[119]

By the end of the eighteenth century it was clear that remains of the (Siberian) mammoth also occurred in North America. They would eventually be found at Big Bone Lick, alongside those of the mastodon, for example. The mastodon itself was confined to the Americas, some specimens occurring in Peru. Both species were adapted for living in cold climates. The mastodon was not a carnivore. The shape of the teeth of the mastodon reflected that it fed on much coarser plant material than the mammoth, including branches and leaves as well as grasses. Meanwhile, it had become fairly obvious to most scholars that the mastodon, like the mammoth, was extinct. The great French zoologist Georges Cuvier, successor to Buffon, pronounced it impossible that creatures so large could have evaded notice, even in the wilds of western North America. But Jefferson never agreed. He had spelled out his argument in *Notes*, and he never deviated from this quite religious view of the inviolate continuity of Nature.

· · ·

Jefferson's comments on the incognitum/mammoth/mastodon in his *Notes* were his first venture into writing about fossils. A decade later, a second opportunity presented itself, and once again Jefferson seized upon a set of fossil remains as possible proof of the existence in America of a mammal of great size and ferocity. Once again he believed (or at least he hoped) that it was still living somewhere in the unexplored West. And once again he hoped that it would be a symbol of American power and authority. Instead of an elephant, this one seemed to be a gigantic kind of lion. It had huge claws, and Jefferson called it the "great-claw" or *Megalonyx*. These new fossils were collected in present-day Greenbriar County, West Virginia, in one of the many limestone caves of that region that were mined for saltpeter. Saltpeter was used in the munitions industry, being one of the three ingredients (with powdered charcoal and sulphur) of black powder. When John Stuart, a former member of the Virginia House of Delegates, heard about the fossils, he sent them to Jefferson, sure that he would find them interesting. "Observing by your Notes your very curious desire for Examining into the antiquity of our Country, I thought the Bones of a Tremendous Animal of the clawed kind … might afford you some amusement … (it is) probably of the Lion kind … The Claw I send must have been one of the Shortest for the man who owns the cave assures me he had one of the same kind that measured precisely eight Inches in Length."[120]

This was an exciting development for Jefferson, one that he could use as further evidence against Buffon (a subject that he evidently did not intend to let drop). Stuart's thought that it seemed to be "of the lion kind" particularly caught his attention. If these were remains of a new kind of predator, it must have been huge. The "animals must have been as preeminent over the lion, as the big buffalo [mastodon] was over the elephant…. The bones are … an evidence against the pretended degeneracy of animal nature in our continent…."[121]

Lying in their protective tray at the Academy of Natural Sciences of Philadelphia, the remains of the great-claw seem meager compared with the interest they stirred up two hundred years ago, but they are still impressive. Stuart had sent the bones of one forelimb and part of the forefoot. The curved toe bones were not the actual claws; they had been enclosed in a horny claw exactly as in a modern dog or cat, but that horny part had long since been lost, leaving the bony core. Jefferson, who had hopes of obtaining further material from West Virginia, sent a letter to the American Philosophical Society about the great-claw, promising to give the fossils to the Society. He then wrote out a memoir on the bones and in March 1797 sent it to the Philosophical Society. The Society then resolved to have the bones studied further. That Jefferson had time for all this is quite amazing, given that he had also just come out of retirement and reluctantly run for president. As runner-up in the voting he became vice president, taking office in March 1797. At the very same time, he accepted the presidency of the American

Philosophical Society where he succeeded Benjamin Rush, to whom he wrote about the great-claw: "What are we to think of a creature whose claws were 8. Inches long, when those of the lion are not 1½ I.?"[122]

When it came to finally publishing his memoir on the great-claw, Jefferson was placed in a terrible quandary, one that brought him close to actual deception. He had never known for certain that the great-claw was a kind of American lion (one such would be discovered forty years later). In his original manuscript he referred to his fossils as being of "the family of the lion, tiger, panther, &c." but changed that to Stuart's phrase "a very large animal of the clawed kind." He still made all his comparisons with the African lion. "These bones only enable us to class the animal with the unguiculated quadrupeds [by which he meant animals with claws] and of these the lion being nearer to him in size, we will compare him with that animal." Jefferson presented tables of comparative measurements,

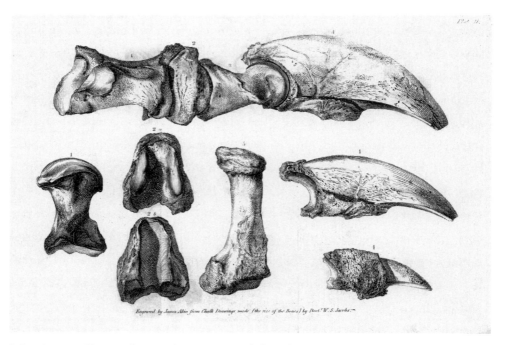

Megalonyx jeffersoni *(great-claw specimens) from Thomas Jefferson, "Memoir on the discovery of certain bones of a quadruped of the clawed kind in the western parts of Virginia,"* Transactions of the American Philosophical Society, *1799 (Ewell Stewart Library, Academy of Natural Sciences)*

concluding: "We may safely say that he was more than three times as large as the lion: that he stood pre-eminently at the head of the column of clawed animals as the mammoth stood at that of the elephant, rhinoceros, and hippopotamus, and that he may have been as formidable an antagonist to the mammoth as the lion to the elephant."[123]

The reason that Jefferson changed his manuscript was that, in fact, he knew that the great-claw was not a kind of lion. In a copy of the periodical *The Monthly Magazine and British Register* that he saw in a Philadelphia book shop there was a drawing showing the reconstruction of a magnificent new fossil found near Buenos Aires.[124] The remains had been put together as a mounted skeleton at the museum in Madrid and studied by Cuvier. It had been given the name *Megatherium* (giant mammal). Like Jefferson's *Megalonyx*, the South American animal was huge. The remains were quite complete, with great claws but, unfortunately, one could see that it was not a lion. It was a giant sloth. A sloth, of course, is the very opposite of a lion, being herbivorous and legendarily passive. So Jefferson added a postscript to his paper in which he acknowledged, rather grudgingly, the double blow—that his great-claw was a species of "slow claw" and that the Europeans had got there first. Nonetheless, Jefferson was able to take a swipe at Buffon in the form of a gracious concession with a little sting in its tail. "Are we from all these to draw a conclusion, the reverse of that of M. de Buffon. That nature, has formed the larger animals of America, like its lakes, its rivers, and mountains, on a greater and prouder scale than in the other hemisphere? Not at all, we are to conclude that she has formed some things large and some things small, on both sides of the earth for reasons which she has not enabled us to penetrate; and that we ought not to shut our eyes upon one half of her facts, and build systems on the other half."

As for whether the animal was still alive somewhere in America, Jefferson repeated his conviction that extinction did not occur in the natural world. But this time he argued rather legalistically on behalf of the great-claw and started off with an acknowledgment that there was a problem. "A difficult question now presents itself. What is become of the great-claw. Some light may be thrown on this by asking another question. Do the wild animals of the first magnitude in any instance fix their dwellings in a thickly inhabited region? Such, I mean, as the elephant, the lion, the tyger? As far as my reading and recollections serve me, I think they do not: but I hazard the opinion doubtingly, because it is not the result of full enquiry." Jefferson hoped the great-claw, like the mastodon, might still be living in the remoter parts of the West. Jefferson's concluding argument was pure rhetoric: "The bones exist, therefore the animal has existed. The movements of nature are in a never-ending circle. The animal species which has once been part of a train of motion, is still probably moving in this train. For if one link in nature's chain might be lost, another one and another might be lost, till this whole system of things should evanish by piece-meal; a conclusion not warranted by the local disappearance of one or two species of animals, and opposed by the hundreds and thousands of instances of the renovating power constantly exercised by nature for the reproduction of all her subjects, animal, vegetable, and mineral. If this animal has once existed, it is possible that he still exists."

Oddly, there is a sort of double postscript to Jefferson's memoir. Jefferson did not mention the fact that, when he had been in Paris in 1789, the American consul in Madrid, William Carmichael, had sent him a note about the fossil sloth from South America and even included a sketch of the bones.[125] Carmichael reported that "He must belong to one of the three largest Quadrupeds, or to the Elephant, Hippotamus or Rhinoceros." The information arrived while Jefferson was packing to return to America. Jefferson brought the papers back with him, but evidently he either forgot about them or did not think that they referred to the same animal.[126] In fact, the sketch does not show the all-important claws. It shows all the parts that were missing from the Greenbriar County material but nothing to link it directly to the great-claw.

While Jefferson's *Megalonyx* might have been a disappointment in terms of American martial pride, the great-claw soon turned out to be the focus of a distinct scientific triumph. The American Philosophical Society had turned the bones over to Caspar Wistar to make a thorough scientific description, and Wistar's paper on the subject was published in the same volume of the *Transactions of the American Philosophical Society* as Jefferson's. Wistar tactfully showed that *Megalonyx*

MEGATHERIUM. *Pl. 1.*

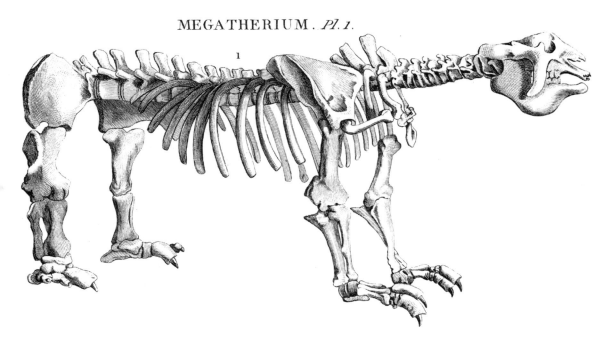

Megatherium from Georges Cuvier, Recherches sur les ossemens fossils de quadrupeds, *1812 (Ewell Stewart Library, Academy of Natural Sciences)*

was related to, but quite distinct from, *Megatherium,* and he went on to make an extremely modern forensic analysis of the bones.

"From the shortness of the metacarpal [wrist] bones, and the form and arrangement of the other bones of the paw, and also from the form of the solitary metatarsal [foot] bone, it seems probable that the animal did not walk on its toes, *it is also evident that the phalanx was not retracted.*" (In other words it was not a feline, like a cat or a lion). "The particular form of [phalanx] No.2, and its connection with the metatarsal bone, and with No.3, must have produced a peculiar species of flexion in the toes, which, combined with the greater flexion of the last phalanx upon the second, must have enabled the animal to turn the claws under the sole of his feet: from this view of the subject there seems to have been some analogy between the feet of the animal and those of the bradypus—having no specimens of that animal I describe these conclusions from the descriptions of the feet given by M.

Daubenton of the great skeleton found lately at Paraguay".[127] This kind of analysis took paleontology to a new level, beyond anything yet achieved in Europe.

• • •

Unfortunately for Jefferson, Lewis and Clark's western expedition failed to find living mastodons or great-claws, but the fossils remained scientifically fascinating as well as objects of great curiosity. Around 1800, fossil mastodon specimens started to turn up in large numbers in Orange and Ulster Counties in New York State. Whereas the Ohio specimens were found in deep soil and rather decayed, these New York specimens were better preserved, having been enclosed in clay. Jefferson and Caspar Wistar communicated about trying to get hold of a skeleton that turned up at Shawangun, Ulster County, New York, but many bones had been taken by souvenir hunters and the rest belonged to the town fathers, who would not part with any.[128]

At around the same time, Jefferson's friend, fellow scientist, and political supporter Charles Willson Peale learned of another promising specimen from New York State near Newburgh. He borrowed money from the Philosophical Society (Jefferson offered government support too) and proceeded to make a series of excavations in the region, from which three reasonably complete skeletons were collected. A mounted skeleton of one of these mastodons (only the second attempt to fully reconstruct a fossil skeleton, the first being the South American *Megatherium*) became the showpiece of the Peale Museum and a major public sensation. Eventually, after a sorry story of debts and several fires, Peale's museum collections were largely lost but, luckily, the first mounted skeleton had been sold to the museum in Darmstadt, Germany, where it remains today.[129]

The second specimen went on tour in Europe, failing to make as much money as had been hoped. Predictably, promoting the mastodon as a public spectacle meant unearthing the idea that it had been a fierce carnivore, and Charles Willson Peale's son, Rembrandt, to whom he entrusted a good deal of the display and publicity of the mastodon, decided that it would best be reconstructed with the tusks curved downwards, rather than upwards. The effect was both dramatic—

the tusks looked like gigantic curved fangs—and ludicrous. Such an animal could not have existed. Rather than being formidable weapons, its tusks would have been in the way of most movements. After scientific opposition was expressed, among others by Rembrandt's son-in-law, the naturalist John Goodman, he eventually restored the tusks to the proper, still quite menacing, position. The question of the diet of the mastodon was finally settled at about the same time, when a specimen was found with a mass of partially ground up plant material in the region of its stomach.[130]

Jefferson was delighted with Peale's successes but still wanted mastodon fossils for his own collections. He may already have had "teeth and bones" that George Rogers Clark collected for him at Big Bone Lick in 1782. [131] He donated a specimen (presumably one of those) to the American Philosophical Society in 1798, and he continued to request "big bones" in the letters that he sent out to friends, asking for zoological specimens of all kinds and particularly big ones. Buffon was still very much on his mind.

In 1803, Charles Willson Peale told Jefferson about a Dr. William Goforth of Cincinnati, who had made a large new collection at Big Bone Lick. Meriwether Lewis, then on his way West for the new Corps of Discovery expedition with William Clark, was dispatched to interview Goforth about getting the collection. Lewis did obtain a tusk and a tooth (probably a tooth of the wooly mammoth, not a mastodon) and these were dispatched to Jefferson. But the boat carrying the bones sank in the Mississippi. Goforth then put his entire collection up for sale and had his agent take it off to England. The man sold it there, absconding with the funds. Sadly, one of the items thereby lost to science was a more or less complete mastodon skull.

Eventually, after the Lewis and Clark expedition had returned, Jefferson commissioned William Clark to go back to Big Bone Lick and make a new collection. Clark reported that the site was by now rather despoiled by collectors, but he managed to make a large haul, rather sensibly being careful to collect small bones as well as the big showy specimens that most of the previous collectors had gone after. "This is probably the most valuable part of the collection, for General Clark, aware that we had specimens of the larger bones, has gathered up everything of the small kind."[132] They found a skull, but it was in very wet deposits where the bones had crumbled too much to be saved. Half of Clark's collection found its way safely to Jefferson in Washington. With it, Clark included the skin of a mountain sheep and an Indian blanket. Clark had, for the sake of safety, divided the collection into two parts. Unfortunately, when forwarded to Jefferson via New Orleans, the second shipment was lost when the ship was impounded in Havana.

Even with only half the collection at hand, so much material arrived at the White House that Jefferson summoned his old friend Caspar Wistar, his colleague at the American Philosophical Society, to Washington to sort the specimens out and divide them up. Jefferson decided to keep a third for himself; Wistar would choose a third for the American Philosophical Society; and the remainder would be donated to the Muséum d'Histoire Naturelle in Paris. Jefferson laid out the fossils—"a precious collection, consisting of upwards of three hundred bones"— on the floor of the unfurnished East Room of the White House, "a large room, where you can work at your leisure, undisturbed by any mortal, from morning till night...."[133] Wistar later described some new species from the Clark collection, including an elk and a bison.[134] Altogether, the swamps at Big Bone Lick have now yielded the remains of seventeen species of large mammals, including mastodon, mammoth, two kinds of bison, two kinds of sloth, two kinds of moose, two kinds of musk ox, elk, caribou, peccary, Virginia deer, black bear, wolf, and a possible tapir.

Jefferson's mastodon specimens were displayed at the White House, and then at Monticello where they had pride of place in the front Hall, along with specimens from the Lewis and Clark expedition. A visitor in 1816 mentioned seeing there "the upper jaw of a mammoth ... from it Mr. Peale made the model with which he completed his mammoth in the Philadelphia museum. The head is complete, but the lower jaw does not belong to the same specimen ... There is also a mammoth's tusk and an elephant's, with a tooth of the latter to show how much it differs from those of the mammoth; the latter being conical and indicating a carnivore, while the other, flat and streaked at the crown, a fructivore." There was also "the head of a gigantic ram; it is supposed that the animal of which it was a part belongs to the primitive race which used to exist in North America."[135]

At his death, Jefferson's collection of mastodon bones, with the rest of his natural history collections, passed to the University of Virginia. Their whereabouts is presently unknown. The American Philosophical Society's specimens were transferred to the Academy of Natural Sciences in Philadelphia, where—with the remains of the great-claw—they are treasured still.

Chapter Seven

Fossils, Shells, and Mountains

In religious terms, Jefferson was a deist, believing that God had made the world and all creation but that nature had been left to run according to its own (God-given) laws after the creation event and without constant divine interference.[136] Jefferson's religious beliefs nonetheless made it hard for him to accept that animals and plants had become extinct in geological times, or to believe that the earth itself had undergone many drastic revolutions that are not described in the Bible, tearing down and rebuilding mountains on a scale far beyond what might have been produced by the forty days and forty nights of Noah's Flood, or even the opening of the "fountains of the deeps."

Jefferson's mastodon and *Megalonyx* fossils were clearly the remains of once living creatures. They were not very old in geological terms, and the environments in which they had been entombed still existed. The most common kinds of fossils in both Europe and America, however, were not bones but fossil seashells. And they had the puzzling habit of occurring high up on mountains.

Leonardo da Vinci had been one of the first in more modern times to ask the question: "Why are the bones of great fishes, and oysters and corals and various other shells and sea-snail,—shells all intermingled, which have become part of [the] stone—[why are they] found on the high tops of mountains...?" In the seventeenth century, it was common to believe that fossil remains had been deposited on mountains by the Great Flood, described in Genesis. Another idea, which Jefferson toyed with very half-heartedly, was that fossils were somehow the creation of the rocks themselves.[137] Some "plastick virtue," in the rocks caused them to make structures mimicking real organisms. Another idea was that somehow ancient seeds had sprouted in the rocks, producing deformed organisms there. Leonardo's answer to the conundrum was very simple: if seashells were found on mountains, then the seas had once covered those mountains. Leonardo observed first that the shells had not been carried into the mountains after their death; "because the years of their growth are numbered upon the outer coverings of their shells; and both small and large ones may be seen; and these would not have grown without feeding, or fed without growing, … and here they would not have been able to move." He dismissed quite contemptuously the notion that fossil shells were produced by the rocks: "if you say that these shells have been and still are being created in such places by the nature of the locality or by the potency of the heavens in these spots, such an opinion cannot exist in brains possessed of any extensive powers of reasoning."[138]

Therefore, Leonardo concluded, it must logically be the case that "The Peaks of the Apennines once stood up in a sea, in the form of islands surrounded by salt water, and above the plains of Italy where flocks of birds are flying today, fishes were once moving in the large shoals."[139] Equally logically, either the seas had retreated to an incomprehensible extent—in which case, where did the water go?—or, after the shells had been deposited in beds on the sea floor, they had been raised up into mountains some equally incomprehensible process. This kind of consideration of the natural history of fossil shells was one of the factors that had led eighteenth-century scholars directly to fundamental questions about the very origins of the earth, its age, and the first configuration of its surface. The central question in the debate concerned the origin of mountains. Various authors had long since established the likelihood that the earth was originally molten, and that, as it rotated, it had settled naturally into the shape of an oblate spheroid rather than a perfect sphere. But that spheroid would presumably have had a flat surface. So, where did mountains come from?

As people explored the surface of the earth, it became more and more clear that it was not in some pristine, perfect state, but seemed in many places to have been violently thrown about. The English cleric Thomas Burnet in his *Telluria Theoria Sacra* (*Sacred History of the Earth*) had observed as early as 1681: "We must … be impartial where the Truth requires it, and describe the Earth as it is really in its self; … 'tis a broken and confus'd heap of bodies, plac'd in no order to one another, nor with any correspondency or regularity of parts: And such a body as the Moon appears to us, when 'tis look'd upon with a good Glass, rude and ragged … a World lying in its rubbish."[140]

Steno, a Danish anatomist and geologist working at the Accademia del Cimento (Academy of Experiments) at Florence in 1669, proposed that the "broken" condition of the earth arose when periods of deposition of strata, laid down one upon the other, were followed by subsidence of the strata into vast underground caverns. The English geologist John Whitehurst proposed that the buildup of superheated steam in caverns under the earth produced great geological catastrophes, "which, bursting the earth, threw it up into mountains and vallies."[141] Robert Hooke (1668) thought the cause was volcanoes and earthquakes and the earth's inner heat. Others credited collisions with comets or held valiantly onto the notion of the Flood. Charles Thomson wrote to Jefferson wondering what the effect might have been of the earth changing the inclination of its orbit to the present 23.5 degrees.

Benjamin Franklin was fascinated by the subject of the origins of the earth's topography. He proposed a remarkably modern explanatory mechanism, supposing "that the internal part (of the earth) might be a fluid … (and that the solid crust) might swim in or upon that fluid. Thus the surface of the earth would be a shell, capable of being broken and disordered by any evident movements of the fluid on which it rested in which the fundamental movements of the earth are driven by its inner heat."[142] This can be read as a fair foreshadowing of the modern theory of plate tectonics, according to which convection currents in the earth's semiliquid inner mantle cause sections of the outer crust (plates) to ride around the surface, bumping into each other and being variously forced upwards, or sucked downwards.

Jefferson's library included a comprehensive set of works on geology and earth history, and he engaged in correspondence with various friends on the subject. He discussed the problems of fossil shells in his *Notes on the State of Virginia*, stating that "Near the eastern face of North mountain are immense bodies of Schist, containing impresions of shells in a variety of forms. I have received petrified shells of very different kinds from the first sources of the Kentucky, which bear no resemblance to any I have ever seen on the tide-waters. It is said that shells are to be found in the Andes, in South America, fifteen thousand feet above the level of the ocean."[143]

In *Notes*, Jefferson considered whether the shells could be evidence of a deluge and used simple calculations to show that no flood of water could ever have been great enough to account for the phenomenon (especially the shells in the high Andes). "A second opinion has been entertained, which is, that, in times anterior to the records either of history or tradition, the bed of the ocean, the principal residence of the shelled tribe, has, by some great convulsion of nature, been heaved up to the heights at which we now find shells and other remains of marine animals." A third solution, for which Jefferson's source was Voltaire, was the old one that nature formed these apparent shells directly in the rocks and was able to inject "the calcareous juice into the form of a shell." Jefferson dryly remarked, "There is a wonder here somewhere." Finding none of the three solutions to the puzzle satisfactory, he left the matter, "Ignorance is preferable to error, and his is less remote from the truth who believes nothing, than he who believes what is wrong." This did not mean, however, that he lost his interest in the matter of shells and mountains. In a letter to David Rittenhouse in Philadelphia, four years later, he summed up his conclusions again. Now he saw four possibilities to account for fossil shells being found on mountains and, as the Rev. James Madison reminded him, on coastal plains.[144] "1. That they have been deposited there by even in the highest mountains by a universal deluge. 2. That they with all the calcareous stones and earths are animal remains. 3. That they grow or shoot as chrystals do.... Another opinion might have been added, that some throw of nature has forced up parts which had been the bed of the ocean. But have we any better proof of such an effort of nature than of her shooting a lapidific juice into the form of a shell?"[145]

For once, Jefferson found himself in a position that he could not resolve either by logic or science. He knew, as a scientist, that there could not have been a great enough deluge to account for all the geological features of the earth. He also knew that theories of a prolonged and violent early history of the earth were at odds with his religious beliefs. It made no sense to him for the Creator to have "made two jobs of his creation," that he "first made a chaotic lump and set it into rotatory motion, and then waiting the millions of ages necessary to form itself, that when it had done this he stepped in a second time to create the animals and plants which were to inhabit it."[146]

As to the geological evidence, Jefferson brought his own observations into the argument. He noted that the strata making up the Blue Ridge and North Mountains of Virginia were deeply folded, often lying more or less vertically, while in the far western country they were reported to lie horizontally. "This variety proves they have not been formed by subsidence as some writers of theories of the earth have pretended.... They may indeed have been thrown up by explosions, as Whitehurst supposes.... But there can be no proof of the explosion, nor is it probable that convulsions have deformed every spot of the earth."[147] By the end of the century, two distinct schools of thought had developed concerning the forces creating and shaping the earth. One of the key issues was to explain the formation of granites. Either the agency had been great heat (the Vulcanist theory) or water (the Neptunist theory). Divisions over these theories were to excite American and European geologists for decades to come. The answer eventually was that both forces had been at work in the earth, but the earth—and granites—had first been molten. Jefferson kept abreast of the latest geological theories, but his interest in this subject was strongest when he was writing his *Notes on the State of Virginia* and when he lived in Paris. He failed to find, either from his own thinking or from the research of others, any solution to these problems. As time went by, he

Table of contents of Notes on the State of Virginia, *copy presented by Jefferson to the American Philosophical Society (American Philosophical Society)*

adopted a somewhat uncharacteristic and even anti-intellectual approach to it all. Having concluded that no useful knowledge could be gained from studying the subject, he simply dismissed it.

In 1805, Jefferson wrote to the French immigrant anthropologist and geographer C.F.C. de Volney that he had not "indulged … in geological inquiries, from a belief that the skin-deep scratches which we can make or find on the surface of the earth, do not repay our time with as certain and useful deductions as our pursuits in some other branches."[148] An even stronger statement came in 1826, with his advice to Dr. John Emmett in reference to a proper curriculum at the University of Virginia: "the dreams about the modes of creation, inquiries whether our globe has been formed by the agency of fire or water, how many millions of years it has cost Vulcan or Neptune to produce what the fiat of the Creator would effect by a single act of will, is too idle to be worth a single hour of any man's life."[149] However, Jefferson's antipathy to speculative geology did not mean that he thought the study of the subject or of mineralogy was a waste. He continued to argue that these branches of science were central to a young person's education.

Chapter Eight

Peoples

A central part of Buffon's theory of American degeneracy was that the indigenous peoples were physically and morally degenerate, weak, and incapable of higher feelings. In this, he was eagerly followed by Abbé Raynal, Corneille de Pauw, and others in Europe. De Pauw said that, "At the time of the discovery of America, its climate was unfavourable to most quadrupedal animals … [and] injurious to the natives who, to an astonishing degree, are stupefied, enervated, and vitiated in all parts of their organism." The "physical faculties" of the American peoples were "basically corrupt [which] had caused the loss of moral faculties. Degeneracy had affected their senses and their organs, and their moral character had suffered to the same extent as their bodies. When Europeans arrived in the West Indies in the fifteenth century, they found not one single American who could read or write; even today there is not one who can think." [150] But Jefferson had a ready answer. In *Notes on the State of Virginia*, he used the same kind of argument by example as he had with respect to the moose and the mastodon. In defense of the Indians of North America (he did not speak for the rest of the New World), he cited a single speech made in 1774 by the "Shawanee Indian," Chief Logan:

"I appeal to any white man to say, if ever he entered Logan's cabin hungry, and he gave him not meat; if ever he came cold and naked, and he clothed him not. During the course of the last long and bloody war, Logan remained idle in his cabin, an advocate for peace. Such was my love for the whites, that my countrymen pointed as they passed, and said, 'Logan is the friend of white men.' I had even thought to have lived with you, but for the injuries of one man, Col. Cresap, the last spring, in cold blood, and unprovoked, murdered all the relations of Logan, not sparing even my women and children. There runs not a drop of my blood in the veins of any living creature. This called on me for revenge. I have sought it: I have killed many; I have fully glutted my vengeance. For my country, I rejoice at the beams of peace. But do not harbour a thought that mine is the joy of fear. Logan

Natural Bridge, *J. C. Stadler, engraver, copy after William Roberts, 1808 (Thomas Jefferson Foundation)*

never felt fear. He will not turn on his heel to save his life. Who is there to mourn for Logan?—Not one." [151]

Jefferson had been genuinely moved by the murders and Chief Logan's speech. The affair had started in early 1774, when two Indians robbed a settler on the western Virginia frontier. Colonel Cresap (actually a Captain), who was already notorious for killing Indians, set out for revenge. When a "canoe of women and children, with one man only," was spotted on the Kanhaway River, Cresap and his men ambushed and killed them all. They were Chief Logan's entire family. Eventually, after battles with the "Shawanees, Mingoes, and Delawares" (Lord Dunmore's War), peace was declared and Logan—who was far from being some degenerate barbarian—delivered his famous speech. The full story of Logan, Cresap, and the relentless pressure that settlers and land speculators (Jefferson and Washington among them) were putting on the Indians and their lands, was much more complicated than Jefferson portrayed in *Notes*. [152] Nonetheless, the speech quickly became known in Europe. It fitted well into Rousseau's view of the noble savage. Even Raynal admired it, and the speech was part of the reason for his withdrawing his earlier claims of American inferiority. "Que cela est beau (how fine it is)," he wrote, "comme celà est simple, energétique et touchant!" [153]

Apparently forgetting that France had been happy to enlist many tribes on their side in the French-Indian wars, and that they had fought well (except insofar as they would change sides), it was Buffon's opinion in 1761 that the American Indian people were naked, feeble, and ignorant. They were as tall as the whites, hardier in the cold, and more agile, but less strong. They were incapable of understanding beauty, love, duty, or honour. They were fearful and cowardly. The "precious spark of the fire of nature has been refused them." Hairless, with small genitals, they lacked sexual virility and had few children. They had no sense of family and the men treated women simply as servants. "Indifference to the other sex is the original effect which blights their nature, prevents its development, and by destroying the germs of life, strikes at the root of society at the same time." [154] In his repetition of these fabrications, repeated enthusiastically by Raynal, it is interesting that Buffon dwelt so lovingly on the matters of sex and procreation. His readers and followers, like William Robertson, also found the whole thing titillating.

Despite being part of the forces that were rapidly driving them to exile and extinction or indeed because of that fact, Jefferson, with his strongly romantic side, had a high regard for the Indians. "Before the Revolution, they were in the habit of coming often and in great numbers to the seat of our government.... I knew much the great Outasseté, the warrior and orator of the Cherokees; he was always the guest of my father, on his journeys to and from Williamsburg. I was in his camp when he made his great farewell oration to his people the evening before his departure for England.... his sounding voice, distinct articulation, animated action, and the solemn silence of his people at their several fires, filled me with awe and veneration, although I did not understand a word he uttered."[155]

Young Chief of the Sack Nation, *circa 1805 (Thomas Jefferson Foundation)*

Outasette, also known as Ostenaco and Austenaco, had fought on the Virginia side in the French-Indian wars and acted as a negotiator for treaties between the British and the Indians.

Buffon did not cite his source for the degeneracy of American wildlife or Indians (presumably it was d'Ulloa). He evidently had not read William Byrd who, in his *Natural History of Virginia*, had written in 1728 that the "Indians are generally tall and well proportioned, which may make full amends for the darkness of their complexions. Add to this that they are healthy and strong, with constitutions untainted by lewdness and not enfeebled by luxury. Besides, morals and all considered, I cannot think the Indians were much greater heathens than the first [European] adventurers."[156] In this, Byrd merely echoed the opinion of Robert Beverley in *The History and Present State of Virginia* (1705): "The *Indians* are of the middling and largest stature of the *English:* They are straight and well proportion'd, having the cleanest and most exact Limbs in the World: They are so perfect in their outward frame, that I never heard of one single *Indian,* that was either dwarfish, crooked, bandylegg'd, or otherwise mis-shapen. Their Colour, when they are grown up, is a Chesnut brown and tawny; but much clearer in their Infancy. Their Skin comes afterwards to harden and grow blacker, by greasing and Sunning themselves ...Their Women are generally Beautiful, possessing an uncommon delicacy of Shape and Features, and wanting no Charm, but that of a fair Complexion." A hundred years later, perhaps the more common view of American Indians was that stated by John Witherspoon in his responses to Barbé-Marbois (for New Jersey). First, he "was never among them." But this did not prevent him from writing that from "all that I have ever heard or read, it appears that the characteristic features of the Indians of North America are that same which have distinguished savages in all parts of the world, and wherever discovered—gravity and sullenness of deportment, love of hunting and war—that is to say, degradation, ferocity to their captives, laziness and aversion to habitual labor, tyranny over the female sex, passive courage, and if it may [be] called so, active cowardice, and strong passions both of lasting gratitude and inextinguishable resentment." Wiitherspoon did not seem to realize that this was, of course, a perfect description of what one might expect of any people who had been dispossessed of their lands and their dignity.[157]

• • •

Jefferson actually *had* spent time among the Indians and could write with authority. In 1781, Jefferson principally knew the Indians of his own state, the "Powhatans, Mannahoacs, and Monacans" who spoke languages "so radically different, that interpreters were necessary when they transacted business." He thought the Monacans were "probably connected with the Massawomecs, or Five Nations ... they partook also of the Tuscarora language. Westward of all these tribes, beyond the mountains, and extending to the Great Lakes, were the Massawomecs.... These were probably the ancestors of the tribes known at present by the name of the Six Nations." The Six Nations were the Mohawks, Oneidas,

Cayugas, Senecas, Onondagas, and Tuscaroras. Jefferson noted that, of the original Virginian peoples, very few were left.[158]

Just as he had with Buffon's arguments about the degeneracy of American animals, in the *Notes*, Jefferson picked off his points one by one, showing their absurdity. Indians were hairless and beardless, for example, not because of a lack of virility but because "with them it is disgraceful to be hairy on the body. They therefore pluck the hair as fast as it appears." This again was confirmed by Beverley: "The Men wear their Hair cut after several fanciful Fashions, sometimes greas'd, and sometimes painted. The Great Men, or better sort, preserve a long Lock behind for distinction. They pull their Beards up by the roots with a Muscleshell; and both Men and Women do the same by the other parts of their Body for Cleanliness sake."[159] Jefferson rejected the idea that these supposedly hairless people showed a reduced sexual ardor (although he unfortunately went on to make the case that "negroes have notoriously less hair than the whites; yet they are more ardent"). If Indians had smaller families than Europeans, it was through economic necessity. When Indian women married white men and were treated well, they produced large families, although it was true that women had a low place in Indian society. They were subjected to "unjust drudgery. This I believe is the case in every barbarous people." Jefferson happily used Buffon's own words against him: even where the Indians lived in those cold wet climates that were supposed to produce degeneracy in animals, they had "essentially the same stature as man in our world." There was ample evidence of the bravery of Indians in battle, and Logan's noble speech was evidence of all the higher sentiments, reflection, and oratory.

Tactfully, Jefferson did not follow Byrd and say that precisely what Buffon and Raynal said about the American Indian could apply equally to poor, illiterate, rural Europeans, and for the same reasons. He did, however, state that sentiment in a private letter written in 1785: "I am safe in affirming that the proofs of genius given by the Indians of N. America, place them on a level with Whites in the same uncultivated state."[160] He also noted that the reason d'Ulloa had found the peoples of South America to be inferior was that they had "passed through ten generations of slavery."[161]

In 1777, Buffon admitted that he had overstated his case, rather disingenu-
ously blaming de Pauw, who had written *after* Buffon's original statements on the
issue, and Peter Kalm for his faulty information.[162] Buffon now concluded that,
because (in translation) "we know from the celebrated Franklin, that in twenty-
eight years the populations of Philadelphia [without immigration] doubled ... in
a country where the Europeans multiply so promptly, where the life of the natives
is longer than previously, it is not possible that humans degenerate."[163]

Interestingly, Jefferson must already have known that Buffon had changed
his position—on humans only—because he owned the *Supplementary Volumes* to
*Histoire Naturell*e. It was there that he had seen Buffon's observations on northern
European cattle, and also the essay (*Epoques de la Nature*) in which Buffon had
outlined his theories of the early history of the earth—something that Jefferson
had been interested in at the time. Buffon thought, with many others of the age,
that the earth had originally been molten and had then cooled. From experiments with molten iron, he made calculations of the possible rate of cooling and
determined that the earth was some 100,000 years old. He also theorized that the
earth's crust was thinner at the two poles and has cooled there more quickly than
at the equator where it is thicker. We know that Jefferson had read these works by
1783 because in January 1784 he dismissed the "inner heat" idea in a letter to James
Madison.[164] Jefferson opposed Buffon's theory, pointing out that the crust would be
cooler where it was thickest (at the equator and on high mountains).

Beyond his responses to Buffon, Raynal, and de Pauw, Jefferson's discussion
of Indians in *Notes* reveals more of his scientific side. He was not interested in the
Indians out of a romantic impulse, or because they were objects of curiosity, and
not even because they presented an almost insuperable obstacle to the westward
expansion of the whites. He wanted to understand them. He asked much the
same questions as did the Europeans, although from a more objective point of
view. Where did Indians come from? What was the significance of all the differences among the tribes, particularly their vastly different languages? What were
the real differences among the Indians, Europeans, and Asians beyond those that

resulted from different circumstances? And what, therefore, were the underlying similarities?

That North American Indians and Asiatic people shared physical resemblances was already well established. Still, the Indians might have come to America from the east, from Norway, via Iceland and Greenland, or from the west, from Siberia. It was the same question that was asked concerning the fauna of North America. Jefferson preferred the idea that American Indians were descended from Asians—with the exception of the Eskimaux (Inuit), whose language showed them to be related to the Greenlanders and therefore, he thought, had come originally from far Northern Europe. This was exactly the opinion that Buffon, quoting Russian explorers, had summarized in his *Supplementary Volume* of 1777.

Jefferson had the insight that patterns of language might be the only secure clues to relationships among all the Indian tribes. He had been fascinated by the Indians and their languages since boyhood when wandering bands of Cherokees still came through Albemarle County. "It is to be lamented ... that we have suffered so many of the Indian tribes already to extinguish ... Were vocabularies formed of all the languages spoken in North And South America, preserving their appellations of the most common objects of nature, of those which must present to every nation barbarous or civilized ... it would furnish opportunities ... to construct the ... derivation of this part of the human race." His view was that for every language in Asia there were twenty in America. For so many languages to have arisen (as he thought) through the gradual modification of a small number of dialects of a single Asiatic language, all diverging from one another "till they have lost all vestiges of their common origin, must require an immense course of time; perhaps not less than many people give to the age of the earth. A greater number of those radical changes of language having taken place among the red men of America, proves them of greater antiquity than those of Asia."[165] In annotations to his own copy of *Notes*, Jefferson speculated as to why this should have happened and tentatively suggested that diversification was a strategy for maintaining the distinctness of groups. He also noted that it might be discovered that there was more in common among the different languages in their terms for numbers than in other words.

By the end of his presidency, Jefferson had collected vocabularies of some fifty different Indian languages, many from the efforts of the Lewis and Clark expedition (Chapter Seven). Some of them he had collected himself, as in the case of the Unquachog people of Long Island. During his 'northern journey" with James Madison, Jefferson had made a special effort to meet the surviving speakers of Unquachog. There were only three older women who knew anything of the language. He recorded two hundred and twelve words, and that is all that now remains of that tongue. Jefferson's vocabularies were intended to be something that he would work on during his retirement years. He would analyze them all and have them printed. Alas, once again distaster struck, just as it had in his early attempts to acquire mastodon fossils and would eventually befall all three of his libraries. The precious vocabularies were all packed into a trunk "and sent round by water with about 30. other packages of my effects from Washington, and while ascending James river, this package, on account of it's weight & presumed precious contents, was singled out & stolen." When the thief discovered that he only stolen some miserable papers, he threw them into the river. "Some leaves floated ashore & were found in the mud; but these were very few, & so defaced … that no general use can ever be made of them."[166] In fact, enough survived, including a sixty-page summary digest, for scholars later to add usefully to the vocabularies of the Mohicans, the Unquachogs, the Shawnee, Oneida, and Delaware.

· · ·

In reply to Barbé-Marbois' enquiry about Indian monuments, Jefferson wrote that he knew of "no such thing existing as an Indian monument; for I would not honour with that name arrow points, stone hatchets, stone pipes, and half-shapen images." But he did, later in the same work, when comparing Indians with the black population, state that they "will often carve figures on their pipes not destitute of design and merit. They will crayon out an animal, a plant, or a country, so as to prove the existence of a germ in their minds which only wants cultivation." This was written before Jefferson had assembled a considerable collection of decorative Indian items of great sophistication, principally brought back to him from western tribes by the Lewis and Clark expedition. But he had already been presented, in 1781, with one or more buffalo skins, painted with elaborate figures by the Kaskaskia chief Jean Baptiste du Coigne, from the Illinois region. Possibly he discounted these artifacts because the chief was of mixed race. These skins have not survived.

In his *Notes*, Jefferson could not point to anything that might indicate shared labor except, as he observed, there were many mounds or barrows in Virginia, some made of earth, some of loose stones, that had been "repositories for the dead." He could make this last statement of their function with authority, as he had personally excavated such a mound in the Rivanna Valley near Monticello. He made a

Jefferson's vocabulary notes (American Philosophical Society)

very systematic, scientific examination of the mound using a vertical trench rather than simply digging in from the top. This allowed him to discover that the barrow had been built with many layers of bones. At the bottom center were stones that had been brought from a cliff a quarter of a mile away. It was clearly a burial site with "very many human bones, at different depths, from six inches to three feet below the surface. These were lying in the utmost confusion." The bones were in poor condition; most were very fragile, although the denser elements such as teeth, jaws, and limb bones were better preserved. The remains were from people of all ages, including children; none showed holes that might have been made by a bullet or an arrow. Although their people had long since been forced west, around 1750 a party of Indians turned up in Albemarle County and went straight to the mound, "through the woods ... without any instructions or enquiry, and having staid about it some time, with expressions which were construed to be those of sorrow, they returned to the high road...."[167]

While Jefferson evidently had a romantic view of the American Indian peoples and admired them, as a scientist he was interested in understanding them in (as it were) their original condition, before being changed by the influence of Europeans. This was a genuine interest that he never lost, even as those days of innocence retreated further and further into the past and became myth. As a politician, on the other hand, he held the hardheaded view that there were only two choices for the Indians: to assimilate or to be destroyed. At first he had had hopes that they could simply be pushed off—albeit with immense suffering and loss—to the West, to compete for a foothold among the tribes already there. He also thought they might find some sort of haven in Canada, especially if the Americans could wrest that land from the British. He had a high regard for those Indians who settled down as agrarians, but he also knew that if they did not assimilate and join his nation of farmers, they would have to be defeated militarily. As had already happened in the East, the lands in the West would, to use the modern phrase, be racially cleansed. The pressure of population growth and westward emigration constituted a force that was unstoppable.

Jefferson's views of the black population, as stated in *Notes*, were distinctly less favorable than his opinions of the Indians. He would not grant that they had any positive attributes at all, other than brute strength and a certain stoicism. The irony of this judgment seems to have escaped him; a slave, especially a field hand, had no choice but to be strong and stoic. He also thought they were inferior "in reason and … incapable … of tracing and comprehending the investigations of Euclid." In imagination they were "dull, tasteless, and anomalous." He thought the sort of oratory demonstrated by Chief Logan was far beyond them, although they were more gifted than whites when it came to music, where their instrument was the "Banjar." He was rudely dismissive of the black poet and classicist Phillis Wheatley (1753–1784), a slave, whose name he misspelled. "Among the blacks is misery enough, God knows, but no poetry." Whereas the Indians might be assimi-

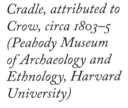

Cradle, attributed to Crow, circa 1803–5 (Peabody Museum of Archaeology and Ethnology, Harvard University)

Knife sheath, attributed to Chippewa/Ojibwa, circa 1803–5 (Peabody Museum of Archaeology and Ethnology, Harvard University)

lated and their intermarriage with whites was not totally condemned, he held out no prospect of the black peoples becoming so embedded in the American nation.

Jefferson did add a caveat to these harsh estimates of character. "To our reproach it must be said, that though for a century and a half we have had under our eyes the races of the black and red men, they have never yet been viewed by us as subjects of natural history. I advance it therefore as a suspicion only, that the blacks, whether originally a distinct race, or made distinct by time and circumstances, are inferior to the whites in the endowments of body and mind. It is not against experience to suppose, that ... varieties of the same species may possess different qualifications." Whether the supposed inferiority of blacks was a false suspicion or true, the product of nature or nurture, and regardless of what the application of natural science to the question might reveal, Jefferson ended this section of *Notes* with a simple flat statement. Noting that other civilizations, such as the Greek and Roman, freed their slaves, he declared that "with us ... when freed [the slave] is to be removed beyond the reach of mixture."[168] Not everyone of that time agreed with such a bleak view of the capacities and potentials of black Americans. Jefferson was roundly criticized in the American Philosophical Society by Samuel Stanhope Smith, president of the College of New Jersey (now Princeton University), in his work of 1787: "An Essay on the Causes of the Variety of Complexion and Figure in the Human Species."[169] Smith stated that Jefferson's judgments had no "foundation in true philosophy" (no scientific basis). Because of the wide circulation of *Notes*, however, Jefferson's views gained currency and helped support common prejudices.

Chapter Nine

NATURAL HISTORY IN THE WEST

Jefferson's *Notes on the State of Virginia* has rightly been hailed as one of the most significant works by an American author of the eighteenth century. In many parts it is a treatise on the whole country, as far as it was then known. But in 1782 a great deal was still unknown. A constant theme in the book, and also in Jefferson's 1799 paper on the great-claw, was his fascination for those wonders that one might discover in the great western sweep of the continent. The West was a symbol of all the things that had fascinated him: both a symbol and a challenge. Traders and explorers had long since talked of that mysterious, bountiful land, with its vast plains and soaring mountains and a richness of animal and plant life very different from anything in the East. Who knew what new crops or mineral resources lay beyond the Appalachians, or the extent of lands for future farming? There, the Indians were still largely (but by no means completely) living their old ways. It was another Garden of Eden, glorious both in its plentitudes and its rawness and violence. But this interest of Jefferson's was by no means romantic. The West was a political plum to be plucked. If it were not made part of the United States, it would forever be a festering sore where other nations such as France, Spain, and Russia could plague the United States. Strong action was needed. Exploration was the prelude to empire. In the process, the returns in the form of natural history would be immense.

In 1783, Jefferson wrote to George Rogers Clark, a Revolutionary War hero and veteran of campaigns towards the West, that an English consortium was raising money for exploring the country from the Mississippi to California. "I am afraid they have thoughts of colonising into that quarter.... Some of us have been talking here in a feeble way of making the attempt to search that country.... How would you like to lead such a party?"[170] It was not until 1786 that Jefferson could try to put any plan into action for promoting the scientific exploration of the West.

He encouraged John Ledyard, a remarkably adventurous explorer who had sailed with Captain Cook to Alaska and had seen the potential for a lucrative fur trade in the Northwest. Ledyard's plan, backed by Jefferson and the Marquis de Lafayette, was to travel by ship to Kamchatka, Russia, and make his way eastward across the Bering Strait to Alaska and the Pacific Coast. Unfortunately, Ledyard was arrested on orders of Catherine the Great and deported. The venture seemed far too much like the spying that it actually was.

Next, in 1792, Jefferson encouraged the American Philosophical Society to back the plans of the French botanist André Michaux to explore northwestward along the Missouri. Michaux was probably more interested in finding new species of trees than in the actual exploration and mapping that interested Jefferson. When this venture was also supported by the French government, it turned out that Michaux had knowingly or unknowingly ventured into a political maelstrom, being accused of stirring up trouble with French settlers and turning them against the Spanish. Once Michaux got to St. Louis, the expedition was aborted.

As previously noted, in 1797, Jefferson had set up a committee of the American Philosophical Society to search for the elusive mastodon. In a 1799 circular from the committee, he requested information also on researches into the "Natural History of the Earth, the changes it has undergone as to Mountains, Lakes, Rivers, Prairies, &c ... [and] to inquire into the Customs, Manners, Languages and Character of the Indian nations, ancient and modern, and their migrations." Jefferson's goal was to encourage western exploration but it was not until he was president and negotiating the Louisiana Purchase (by which the territory of the United States was doubled) that his dreams were realized. Now, at last, was the moment when political interference was very much needed to consolidate the politico-legal situation.

The expedition of Lewis and Clark's "Corps of Northwestern Discovery" is now legendary in the annals of American exploration. In terms of natural history, it was a success, even though it failed to turn up any sign of a living mastodon or great-claw. The man Jefferson chose to lead the expedition of some forty souls turned out to be just what he needed. William Clark was the younger brother of

George Rogers Clark and a junior Army officer. Clark chose Jefferson's secretary, the young Meriwether Lewis, to go with him. Lewis was brave and resourceful and already an accomplished, if raw, naturalist. His mother was an herbal remedist of note, and Lewis knew the plants of the eastern regions well. In preparation, Jefferson arranged for Lewis to go to Philadelphia and learn some of the science that would be useful during the expedition.[171] The astronomer Andrew Ellicot and the mathematician Robert Patterson taught him mapping and surveying. They advised him about instruments to take, including sextants, a chronometer, and compasses. Benjamin Rush, America's greatest physician, taught him the elements (then primitive) of field medicine. Caspar Wistar showed him the kinds of fossils to look for and how to prepare the skins and skeletons of animals they found. Benjamin Smith Barton gave him a crash course in botany. Although Lewis was an experienced field botanist, more would be needed in order to identify the western relatives of eastern plants. Barton showed him how to collect and preserve seeds, and how to press dried leaves, flowers, and whole plants.

The Lewis and Clark team started up the Missouri in May of 1804 and reached the Pacific Ocean in December 1805. They returned to the East in 1806.[172] The expedition was very carefully planned. Jefferson gave outlines of its mission to many colleagues in Washington in advance, for comment. The expedition was commissioned to explore the Missouri River to its source and then to find the best route to the Pacific by discovering a means to transport goods by water from St. Louis to the Columbia River. Science was certainly very high on Jefferson's agenda, but as usual there were other agendas: diplomatic, colonial, and mercantile. The list of things they were charged to observe was nothing less than a summary of everything that had interested Jefferson for his whole life. For the native people they would encounter, Jefferson's instructions to Lewis were to observe: "The commerce which may be carried on with the people inhabiting the line you will pursue, renders a knolege of those people important. You will therefore endeavor to make yourself acquainted, as far as a diligent pursuit of your journey shall admit, with the names of the nations & their numbers; the extent & limits of their possessions; their relations with other tribes of nations; their language, traditions, monuments;

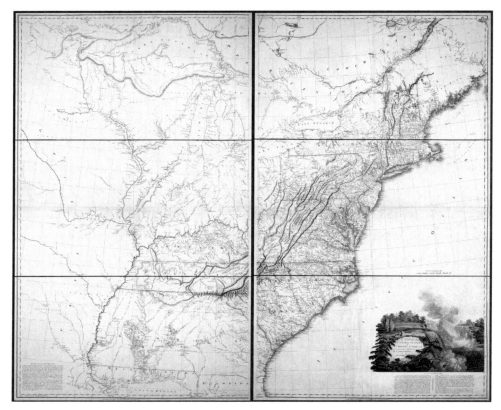

"A Map of the United States of North America," by Aaron Arrowsmith, 1802 (Library of Congress, Geography and Map Division)

their ordinary occupations in agriculture, fishing, hunting, war, arts, & the implements for these; their food, clothing, & domestic accommodations; the diseases prevalent among them, & the remedies they use; moral & physical circumstances which distinguish them from the tribes we know; peculiarities in their laws, customs & dispositions; and articles of commerce they may need or furnish, & to what extent.

And, considering the interest which every nation has in extending & strengthening the authority of reason & justice among the people around them, it will be useful to acquire what knolege you can of the state of morality, religion, & information among them; as it may better enable those who endeavor to civilize & instruct them, to adapt their measure to the existing notions & practices of those on whom they are to operate."

In the natural world, "Objects worthy of notice will be; the soil and face of the country; its growth and vegetable productions, especially those not of the United States, the animals of the country generally, and especially those not known in the United States; the remains and accounts of any which may be deemed rare or extinct; the mineral productions of every kind, but particularly metals, limestones, pit-coal and saltpetre; salines and mineral water, noting the temperature of the last, and such circumstances as may indicate their character; volcanic appearances; climate, as characterized by the thermometer, by the proportion of rainy, cloudy, and clear days, by lightning, hail, snow, ice, by the access and recess of frost, by the winds prevailing at different seasons, the dates at which particular plants put forth or lose their flower or leaf, times of appearance of particular birds, reptiles or insects."[173]

· · ·

The Corps of Discovery was so-named because it was intended to operate within the Doctrine of Discovery which provided that European settlers gained the rights to lands they discovered. Discovery was usually marked by the familiar symbolic planting of a national flag. To plant the flag at the mouth of a river was considered enough to claim its entire watershed—hence the need to proceed to the mouth of the Columbia River. With the Louisiana Purchase, the United States did not buy from France the title to the western lands beyond the Missouri, nor were the western lands "undiscovered" (especially to the Indians). Instead, "the United States bought the Discovery rights to a limited sovereignty over the territory, the right to be the only government the Indian Nations could deal with politically and commercially, and the preemption right, the exclusive option to purchase the real estate whenever the owners, the Indian Nations, chose to sell."[174] The Corps of Discovery was therefore charged to make treaties with the Indian tribes along the route, both by recognizing their sovereignty over their own lands and, in a curious piece of diplomatic nicety, by insisting that the government in Washington was now the Indians' new "fathers." The Indian tribes were sovereign nations, but they were told that they were also subject to the overarching laws and policies of the

*William Clark,
portrait by Charles
Willson Peale, circa
1810 (Independence
National Historical
Park)*

*Meriwether Lewis,
portrait by Charles
Willson Peale, circa 1807
(Independence National
Historical Park)*

United States. Making treaties with them was essential; the alternative was the use of force. Fighting these little-known enemies in an unknown land was not a practical proposition, let alone a moral one. "The Indians can be kept in order only by commerce or war. The former is the cheapest," wrote Jefferson.[175] Over the next 150 years, three hundred million dollars had to be added to the cost of the Louisiana Purchase to buy Indian lands.[176]

The expedition took along a huge amount of trade goods (but still not enough) with which to buy the Indians' compliance, to exchange for artifacts, and to open the way for future traders to follow their path by replacing the French and Spanish traders who had travelled these routes before them. And everywhere, at all times, one of their missions was to collect natural history information about the animals, the plants, the geology, and the peoples. One of Jefferson's other great preoccupations was the Indian languages and customs. He prepared questionnaires so that information could be gathered uniformly about each group the Corps of Discovery encountered. The expedition, and Lewis particularly, recorded a vast amount of information about the various Indian peoples and collected a great number of natural history specimens. Forty different vocabularies were collected. In June of 1804 they sent back a collection of artifacts from the Osage Indians, including an Osage warrior's emblem, and a second shipment of several crates was sent to Jefferson in 1805 from North Dakota. From Lewis's detailed lists of this second group of specimens, we know that there were skins and skeletons from antelope, deer, and prairie dog, horns of elk and mountain sheep, skins of red fox, "yellow" bear, weasel, squirrel and hare, "insects and mice … [and] a Mandan cooking pot." With them, Lewis included "buffalo robes and other apparel of the Mandans and Minitarras [Hidatsas]," one of them painted with a representation of "a battle between the Sioux and Ricars [Arikaras] and the Minetarras and Mandans."[177] This was the painted skin that hung in the Hall at Monticello and was commented upon by every visitor.

Of botanical specimens, Lewis sent to Jefferson boxes containing hundreds of dried plant specimens and boxes of seeds. Among the plants shipped in 1805 were Arikara tobacco seeds (which Jefferson grew at Monticello), an ear of

Mandan corn, and roots of a plant (the prairie cone flower) "highly prized by the natives as an efficacious remedy in Cases of the bite of the rattle Snake or Mad Dog." The roots were still viable when they arrived and Jefferson grew that plant also. In addition, Lewis had also sent to Jefferson some live animals. Most of them were insect pests that had invaded the boxes! Henry Dearborn, secretary of war, inspected the shipment for Jefferson and reported to him that there were "great numbers of vermin."[178] The casks with buffalo robes and animal skins were in fairly good condition; they were aired, brushed with snuff, and packed away. But, most remarkably, the original shipment had also included three cages containing a live prairie dog, four magpies, and a "hen of the prairie." Only the prairie dog and one magpie made it all the way to Washington. Jefferson sent them to Charles Willson Peale for his Philadelphia Museum, along with many of the Indian artifacts and animal skins and skeletons.

Much valuable material never found its way back East, but a final large shipment of collections went to Jefferson after the expedition had returned to St. Louis in 1806. It included material from the Northwest Coast including Clatsop hats, many more pressed dried plants, and rock and mineral samples. Lewis sent Jefferson a further collection of seeds in 1807. Altogether, Lewis and Clark collected 178 species of plants that were named by botanists as new to science (over the years, re-study has reduced the list of distinct species, as opposed to varieties, to about eighty[179]). In addition to the cone-flower already mentioned, the new species included the now familiar Osage orange (the wood of which the Indians used for their bows), purple coneflower, prickly pear, western paper birch, bitterroot, two species of cottonwoods, cut-leaf daisy, Jacob's ladder, red-flowering currant, golden currant, and sagebrush. Most of the forest trees were new. Among the ornamentals were a yellow fritillary, Oregon grape, and lovely snowberry, a bush that is covered with small white berries in the fall.[180]

Jefferson grew the Osage orange at Monticello. Because of the thorny bark of the young trees, it quickly became popular for use in hedges. He also experimented with many of the potential crop plants collected by the expedition, particularly those from the agriculturalist Mandan, Arikara, and Hidatsa tribes.[181]

Of kinds of Indian corn, Jefferson tried growing the Pawnee corn and the Arikara corn in his garden together with the yellow Arikara Bean, Mandan tobacco (a very inferior kind), wild salsify, the "flowering pea of the plains of Arkansas," two species of currant, and gooseberries. All of these were also developed commercially by Bernard McMahon although most turned out not to produce yields as good as established eastern varieties.

Of the animals observed by the expedition, 122 were new species or subspecies, including the prairie dog, grizzly bear, mule deer, pronghorn, magpie, trumpeter swan, western rattlesnake, hognose snake, garter snake, and channel catfish. That these plants and animals now so familiar to us were then unknown in the East is a testimony to the fact that Lewis and Clark had ventured into such new territory (for Europeans, that is).

As the crates from the West arrived in Washington, Jefferson divided up the material. He was far too busy with the presidency to be able to devote very much time to the propagation of the western plants, exciting as they were. While the collections technically were the property of the government, using them and getting them studied by experts required their distribution. Practical skills were needed for propagating the plants and Jefferson sent all the seeds to McMahon and William Hamilton in Philadelphia. From their efforts, a substantial number of western plants came into wide use in the eastern states and many were exported to Europe as well. The dried plants were sent to the American Philosophical Society for Benjamin Smith Barton to examine. Most of the ethnographic material was given to Charles Willson Peale's Museum in Philadelphia. Jefferson kept "an Indian bow and a quiver of arrows, a cooking pot, four buffalo hides and other items of dress," and the big buffalo hide painted with the battle scene of 1797.[182] All the mineral specimens went to the American Philosophical Society.

. . .

While the expedition was a decided success in terms both of exploration and discovery in natural history, it was also something of a disappointment to Jefferson. Lewis and Clark failed to find a ready passage by water from the continental

Page from the Journal of Meriwether Lewis (American Philosophical Society)

interior to the Pacific Ocean. There were no living mastodons or great-claws and, although the bounty of new species of animals and plants would occupy naturalists for decades to come, the results were not made known to the public immediately. After various miscues and the untimely death of Lewis, it was not until 1814 that an account of the expedition was published.[183] Meanwhile, Jefferson's political enemies lambasted his expedition as a conspicuous waste of money.

Like Jefferson's libraries, his fossils, and his Indian vocabularies, the majority of the scientific specimens collected by Lewis and Clark were eventually lost. Many of the mineral specimens that were given to the American Philosophical Society for study by Dr. Adam Seibert later went to the Academy of Natural Sciences in Philadelphia (founded 1812), but were incorporated with the rest of Seibert's own collection, and only a few can now be identified. The zoological and ethnographic material sent to Peale's museum was mostly destroyed in various fires, although a small amount of this material eventually found its way to the Peabody Museum at Harvard. Specimens that can definitely be identified with Lewis and Clark include three Sioux raven belts, an otter bag, two basket-weave whalers' hats from the Nootka or Makah of the Northwest, and a bear-claw necklace. Other specimens at Harvard that might have come from the expedition, either directly or via Jefferson, include "a Mandan eagle-bone whistle and buffalo robe, a Sac and Fox tobacco pouch, a flute from the northern Plains Indians ... a Crow cradle, and an Ojibwa knife."[184] The Museum of Comparative Zoology at Harvard has the skin of Lewis's "black woodpecker."

Lewis found a number of fossils during the trip. One of the first was a specimen later labeled "Jawbone of a fish or some other animal found in a Cavern a few miles distant from the Missouri." The journals record discovery of fossil wood, shells, and remains of a large reptile (ribs, vertebrae) that might have been a plesiosaur, a mosasaur, or even a dinosaur. Only the fish jaw bone survives; it is now named *Saurocepahlus lanciformis*. The dried plants had an even more checkered history and only 238 of the sheets of dried specimens survive. Lewis had originally wanted to write a book on the plants with the help of Benjamin Smith Barton. But Lewis died, mysteriously, in 1809 and Barton followed him in 1815.

Before Barton's death, some of the sheets of dried plants were loaned to Jefferson's plantsman friend Bernard McMahon. The German botanist Frederick Pursh was then in Philadelphia variously working with Hamilton and McMahon, hoping to write a great book on the American flora.[185] The temptation presented by this spectacular collection of new plants must have been too great. He stole some fifty of the sheets and took them to England. There, working for a new patron, Aylmer Lambert, a noted botanical scholar and collector, Pursh described some ninety-four new forms based on Lewis and Clark specimens in his book *Flora Americae Septentrionalis* (1813) and acknowledged his sources by naming two new genera: *Lewisia* and *Clarkia.* The sheets of specimens that he had taken stayed in London with Lambert and, on his death, were sold at auction and eventually ended up at the Academy of Natural Sciences of Philadelphia. The sheets (including those for *Lewisia* and *Clarkia)* that had remained in Philadelphia, in the attic of the American Philosophical Society, were also eventually passed on to the Academy of Natural Sciences of Philadelphia for safekeeping.[186]

Chapter Ten

NATURE AND THE MAN

Thomas Jefferson is, as Joseph Ellis has memorably described him, something of a "sphinx." Just when we think we have neatly categorized him, he surprises us—and sometimes disappoints us—with new twists and turns of character and unexpected enthusiasms.[187] With his passion for detailed knowledge, precise calculations, and rational enquiry, he was very much a product of the Enlightenment. Yet, throughout, there is a strong counter theme of romanticism. While his vegetable gardens and orchards were laid out in strict rows and squares, his pleasure gardens were informal and picturesque. His farming was scientific, but the views from his property were enhanced to create the sublime. He was very much a man of ideas but with strict limits. True to his credo that all knowledge and ideas must yield useful results, he drew a clear line between productive ideas and "idle" speculation.

For Jefferson the science of natural history was never an abstraction, divorced from day-to-day affairs. It related to everything he did, as a farmer, as a philosopher, and as a citizen. Jefferson had been taught well by William Small at the College of William and Mary. All knowledge, all discourse, all enquiry, must be based in facts. There is only one nature; discussion of a non-natural or supra-natural world or of myths, spirits, and miracles, was not rational. Rational thinking was the goal of any educated person. Natural history, in this view, is more than a set of facts about nature and nature itself; it is something larger still, verging on the symbolic rather than the material.[188] In Jefferson's personal philosophy, nature, the "what is" of the world, was the source of all that was good.

Part of the Enlightenment view of physical nature was that it would (eventually) be revealed as orderly and predictable, governed by natural laws. The most striking of those were the laws of motion and gravity discovered by Newton. Human nature must also be governed by natural laws. And if there were natural laws, then there are natural rights. All of this became a central part of Jefferson's political philosophy. It was a fundamental fact of nature that all men are created equal, and a whole suite of rights and responsibilities flowed from that fact. If natural philosophy (science) were to establish beyond doubt that all humans were not created equal—and this would be a long-standing issue right until the time of Charles Darwin and beyond—then rights (and again responsibilities) for different groups would be different. And that would create—and periodically has done so—a long, slippery road to human misery.

Natural history (the facts about animals, plants, and minerals) and the broader concept of nature (the all-encompassing set of properties inherent in, and resulting from, the material properties of the world) were for Jefferson a continuum. One could not understand and analyze one without the other. Beyond natural law and natural rights, one other major idea concerned the minds of scholars contemporary with Jefferson. "Natural theology" was the concept that, because God created all nature, a study of nature is a way of coming closer to understanding God's mind and his purposes for man on earth. In this view, the more one finds order and lawfulness in nature, through systems like Linnaeus' classification, for example, or through the discovery of physical laws, the more one approaches a view of the symmetry and rationality of God's mind. This was an important antidote to the view that God, by performing miracles at will, could violate the laws of nature. One of Galileo's heresies, it will be remembered, was that he would not admit that God had made the sun move backward in the sky as reported in the Bible.

A critical feature of natural theology was the analysis and explanation of the adaptations of living organisms to their environments: the long beak of the hummingbird for probing into flowers, the strong beak of the woodpecker for excavating insects from trees, the pouch of the pelican for holding food, and so on. Adaptation was therefore an example of the purpose that God had for all his creation, for whom that purpose is often hard to discern when God has also, apparently, created evil, pestilence, sickness, and death both in the human and non-human world. Jefferson had a purer view of such matters. As a deist he believed that God created the world and also created its laws, such as the law of gravity, by which it operated like some immensely elaborate machine. But having done so,

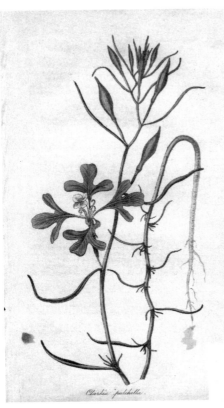

Lewisia rediviva, Curtis's
Botanical Magazine, *1863 (Ewell
Stewart Library, Academy of
Natural Sciences)*

Clarkia pulchella *from
Frederick Pursh,* Flora Americae
Septentrionalis, *1816 (Ewell
Stewart Library, Academy of
Natural Sciences)*

God left nature to run its own course. Another fallacy that Jefferson avoided was the utilitarian view that everything in nature is created for man's use. The extreme of this view would be that the sea is salt in order to flavor our cooking and the tides exist to float our ships in and out of harbor, and so on.

Jefferson's philosophy was much more completely grounded. It began, as it had in his boyhood, with a thorough knowledge and experience of nature in the natural world itself. He was a countryman, even when working at the highest levels of government in America and in Europe's greatest cities. This marked him and his philosophy of life and of government as different from his contemporaries in Paris, London, or even Philadelphia and Boston. He long held Saxon-era Europe as a model for what a society *should* be. In Jefferson's idealized view, before the Norman Conquest brought to England a concept of a single king, lords, and a feudal system of government, the Saxons were "a set of people who lived freely and harmoniously, without kings or lords to rule over them, working and owning their land as sovereign agents."[189] These mythical farmers were Jefferson's ideal. "Those who labour in the earth are the chosen people of God…."[190] His perfect nation would be made up of yeoman farmers. "Cultivators of the earth are the most valuable citizens."[191]

Jefferson never completely lost this conviction that to be a farmer was life's highest calling and that the nation would be best served if her people were not trapped in the mercantilism of the cities. That would, of course, have been a naively romantic view and Jefferson was far too sophisticated to succumb to it. As he came to realize, even before he had been born, history had become entrained in ways that made such dreams impossible. Cities, industry, and commerce were as inevitable (and important) as agriculture was essential.[192] Nonetheless, the creation of a romantic, quasi-wilderness retreat carved out of the mountaintop wilderness, and juxtaposed more or less uneasily with a working plantation and slaves, seems in every way to fit with Jefferson's fascination (almost an obsession) with the notion of a more perfect world represented by Europe in the first millennium. Monticello was the first American Camelot.

Jefferson's natural history and his views of the grander sweep of nature were always as contradictory as the rest of his life. He was both a romantic and a practical farmer; he both admired the Indians and helped annihilate them; he believed that all men were created equal but was not sure about the black people; he believed that all men should be free and was generous and benevolent to his slaves, but he could not emancipate them. He was, in short, an idealist caught, as we all are, in the web of his times. But, more than most, he stayed true to his main anchor: living nature and the land. He was a hard-edged realist about natural history. He was the man, after all, who could calculate precisely the amount of hay one horse would eat in a winter. But he was also the man who could write to Maria Cosway about seeing in nature elements of the sublime—a transcendental beauty and power. Perhaps that was not a contradiction, after all.

APPENDICES

Appendix A: Jefferson's Name in Natural History

Given Jefferson's early enthusiasm for the Linnaean system of nomenclature for plants and animals, it is appropriate that his name has been formally enshrined in biology in the names of several species. Perhaps Jefferson, with his familiarity with the classical languages, would now be amused at the kinds of names that biologists have coined in his honor.

The list (probably incomplete) of eponymous animals starts with the two species of the fossils most famously associated with Jefferson. *Megalonyx jeffersoni* is the giant sloth species that Jefferson nicknamed the 'great-claw.' *Mammuthus jeffersoni* is a mammoth fossil sometimes demoted to the subspecies, *Mammuthus columbi jeffersoni*. Less well-known fossil species are *Baioconodon jeffersoni*, a (Paleocene) relative of very early mammals; *Douglassia jeffersoni*, the oldest known (late Eocene) fossil squirrel; *Boreogomphodon jeffersoni*, another kind of extinct mammal called a traversodont; and *Teredinia jeffersoni*, a fossil boring bivalve.

The most famous of the living animals named for him is the Jefferson salamander, *Ambystoma jeffersonianum*, from the Eastern United States. A second salamander named for Jefferson is the rare Blue Ridge Seal salamander, *Desmognagthus jeffersoni*. A subspecies of the American badger, *Taxidia taxus jeffersoni*, is endangered in Canada (and also occurs, with *Mammuthus jeffersoni*, as a fossil at the Rancho La Brea Tar Pits in California).

After that, the eponymous species become less conspicuous, including a number of living animals and plants that are mostly known only to specialists: *Orconectes jeffersoni*, a crawfish; *Rhipodocotyle jeffersoni* and *Pararhipidocotyle jeffersoni*, parasitic worms; *Brachypanorpa jeffersoni*, a mecopteran insect (Jefferson's short-nosed scorpion fly, endangered); *Dendryphantes jeffersoni*, a spider; *Floridinella jeffersoni*, a byrozoan; and *Dicodonium jeffersoni*, a jellyfish relative.

The best-known plant named for Jefferson is the rare, but lovely, twinleaf, *Jeffersonia diphylla*, flowering on limestone soils in the springtime woods of eastern North America. A cultivated variety of camelia and a variety of wheat are named for Jefferson, along with a subspecies of the Midland shooting star, *Dodecatheon meadis jeffersoni*. The final honor, or perhaps indignity, rests with *Triphragmiopsis jeffersonae*—a fungus that causes brown rust of larch trees. In addition, there is a mineral, *Jeffersonite*, a dark green magnesium-zinc inosilicate found first at Franklin Mines, New Jersey. And twenty-four cities in the United States are named "Jefferson," as are twenty-five counties and one parish.

Appendix B

Letter of the Marquis de Barbé-Marbois, accompanying his questionnaire (as received by Chief Justice McKean of Delaware)*

Sir,
I take the liberty to state to you some questions relative to the State of Delaware. I know how precious is your time and wish to distract you as little as possible from your public affairs. But you will greatly oblige me if in some leisure hour you could give me some answers to these questions and if there are any which cannot be answered with certainty I beg that you would be so obliging as to send them to some person in the State of Delaware, who you think will be disposed to answer them. I am drawing up a memoir respecting the 13 United States in general and each one in particular, and therefore wish to have exact accounts respecting that of Delaware.

I am, sir, Your humble and very obedient servant
De Marbois

---

* Historical Society of Pennsylvania, McKean Papers. Translated, KST

Appendix C

The questionnaire of the Marquis de Barbé-Marbois

Articles of which you are requested to give some details

1. The Charters of your State.
2. The present Constitution.
3. An exact description of its limits and boundaries.
4. The Memoirs published in its name, in the time of its being a Colony and the pamphlets relating to its interior or exterior affairs, present or ancient.
5. The History of the State.
6. A notice of the Counties Cities Townships Villages Rivers Rivulets and how far they are navigable. Cascades Caverns Mountains Productions Trees Plants Fruits and other natural Riches.
7. The number of its Inhabitants.
8. The different Religions received in that State.
9. The Colleges and public establishments. The Roads Buildings &c.
10. The Administration of Justice and a description of the Laws.
11. The particular Customs and manners that may happen to be received in that State.
12. The present state of Manufactures Commerce interior and exterior Trade.
13. A notice of the best Sea Ports of the State and how big are the vessels they can receive.
14. A notice of the commercial productions particular to that State and of those objects which the Inhabitants are obliged to get from Europe and from other parts of the World.
15. The weight measures and the currency of the hard money. Some details relating to the exchange with Europe.
16. The public income and expences.
17. The measures taken with regard of the Estates and Possessions of the Rebels commonly called Tories.

18. The condition of the Regular Troops and the Militia and their pay.

19. The marine and Navigation.

20. A notice of the Mines and other subterranean riches.

21. Some samples of these Mines and of the extraordinary Stones. In short a notice of all what can increase the progress of human Knowledge.

22. A description of the Indians established in the State before the European Settlements and of those who are still remaining. An indication of the Indian Monuments discovered in that State.

ACKNOWLEDGEMENTS

I am grateful to Daniel Jordan, president of the Thomas Jefferson Foundation, and Andrew O'Shaughnessy, director of the International Center for Jefferson Studies (ICJS), for inviting me to write this book and for extending the privilege of a visiting fellowship at Monticello in the fall of 2007.

Nothing I have ever written has been possible without the support of libraries, and I would not have dreamt of taking on this task without the help of the research libraries at Monticello, at the American Philosophical Society, and at the Academy of Natural Sciences of Philadelphia. I am particularly grateful to Eric Johnson and Anna Berkes (ICJS), Marty Levitt and Roy Goodman (APS), and Elaine Matthias and Mary-Gen Davies (ANSP) for their personal assistance and advice. Sara Bon-Harper, Leni Sorenson, Gaye Wilson, Susan Stein, Mary Scott-Fleming, and many others at Monticello, not forgetting fellow Fellows Monica Henry and Mathew Hale, provided assistance and encouragement. Peter Hatch, the supreme expert on Jefferson's gardens at Monticello (and much else) helped just when I needed it. Joan Hairfield made my wife and me wonderfully welcome during our delightful stay on Jefferson's little mountain.

Andrew O'Shaughnessy, Peter Hatch, Leni Sorenson, Robert McCracken Peck, Gaye Wilson, Ernest Schuyler, Andrea Wulf, Susan Stein, and Linda Price Thomson generously read all or part of the manuscript and made valuable comments and corrections.

Abbreviations used in Endnotes

L&B—*The Writings of Thomas Jefferson*, Andrew A. Lipscomb and Albert Ellery Bergh, eds. Washington, D.C.: Thomas Jefferson Memorial Association, 1903. This compilation is very incomplete but useful for letters written after 1811.

Garden Book—*Thomas Jefferson's Garden Book*, Edwin Morris Betts, ed. Philadelphia: American Philosophical Society, 1944.

Papers—*The Papers of Thomas Jefferson*, Julian Boyd, ed. Princeton: Princeton University Press, 1950, ongoing.

Retirement—*The Papers of Thomas Jefferson, Retirement Series*, J. Jefferson Looney, ed. Princeton: Princeton University Press, 2004, ongoing. These volumes cover the years 1809 onward.

Notes—Thomas Jefferson, [1787] *Notes on the State of Virginia*, Frank Shuffleton, ed. New York: Penguin Books, 1999.

TJ—Thomas Jefferson as the writer or recipient of correspondence

ENDNOTES

Notes to Chapter One, pages 9–21

1   The Blue Ridge is part of the Appalachian mountain chain stretching from Alabama to New England. Geographers call the type of landscape in Albemarle County "piedmont" (foot of mountain). It is marked by rolling hills and generally a higher relief than the more lowland country to the east or, of course, the Virginia tidewater country.

2   TJ to Baron Geismar, September 6, 1785, *Papers*, 8: 499–500.

3   Paul Leicester Ford, ed., *The Autobiography of Thomas Jefferson, 1743–1790* (Philadelphia: University of Pennsylvania Press, 2005), 1–2.

4   Peter Collinson in Rodney Howard True, "Thomas Jefferson in Relation to Botany," *Scientific Monthly* 3 (1916): 347.

5   TJ to John Page, February 21, 1770, *Papers*, 1: 34–36.
Among the books that were important in Jefferson's early education in natural history was *Flora Virginica* (1743, revised in 1762 by Gronovius from a manuscript by John Clayton, a long-time English resident of Gloucester County). Clayton was a friend of the family and Jefferson obtained seeds from him. Mark Catesby's *Natural History of Carolina, Florida and the Bahama Islands* (1731–1743) and Peter Kalm's *Travels into North America* (1770) were two of the foremost references on the animals and plants of North America. This first Jefferson library would surely also have owned Robert Beverley's *The History and Present State of Virginia*, with its descriptions of geography, natural history, the Indians, and also Virginia's political structures and laws. In his ideas about gardening—a lifelong passion—Jefferson was also strongly influenced by Thomas Whately's *Observations on Modern Gardening* (1770) which discussed the great formal gardens of Britain. But the most influential works were by Philip Miller, perhaps England's most notable gardener of the century. Jefferson owned Miller's *The Gardener's Dictionary* (published 1731 with many later editions) and *The Gardener's Kalendar* (1732) and made many references to them over the years in his memorandum book and diary known as the Garden Book. Miller (1691–1771) was the superintendent of Chelsea Physic Garden, London. His *Gardener's Dictionary* was revolutionary for its time and was the first modern work on practical horticulture for both the professional and the home enthusiast. While other botany books of the day consisted of formal descriptions of plants, Miller, building on his own experiences, offered "methods of cultivating and improving the kitchen, fruit and flower-garden. As also, the physick garden, wilderness, conservatory and vineyard … Interspers'd with the history of the plants, the characters of each genus, and the names of all the particular species, in Latin and English, and an explanation of all the terms used in botany and gardening." The book was immensely influential in bringing together horticulture and scientific natural history. Miller's work was supplanted in later years by the home-grown *The American Gardener's Calendar* (1806) by Bernard McMahon.

6   TJ to George Washington, June 28, 1793, *Papers*, 26: 396–98.

7   Ford, *The Autobiography of Thomas Jefferson*, 5–6. Small soon returned to Britain, moving to Birmingham where he became a part of the coterie of brilliant inventors, thinkers, and business-men known as the Lunar Men (they met at the full moon so as to have well-lit nights for their journeys home). Among these men were the doctor, poet, and scientific philosopher Erasmus Darwin (the grandfather of Charles Darwin and well known as an early proponent of evolu-tionary theories), the manufacturers Josiah Wedgwood and Matthew Boulton, and the engineer James Watt, famous for his work on steam engines. True to the spirit that he inculcated in

Jefferson and other pupils, Small combined his love of both pure and useful knowledge, joining Boulton in his Soho Engineering Works.

8   Some of these food plants had had a circuitous history: the potato, sweet potato, and pumpkin, for example, originated in the New World, were grown in the Old World, and then those cultivars were reintroduced to the Americas.

9   TJ to George Gilmer, August 12, 1787, *Papers*, 12: 24–26.

10 *Garden Book*, 4.

11 *Garden Book*, 5.

12 *Jefferson's Memorandum Books*, vol. 1, James A Bear, Jr. and Lucia C. Stanton, eds. (Princeton: Princeton University Press, 1997), 387.

13 TJ to Mary Jefferson, June 13, 1790, *Papers*, 16: 491–92.

14 Mary Jefferson to TJ, ca. August 11, 1790, *Papers*, 17: 332–33.

15 TJ to Mary Jefferson, March 9, 1791, *Papers*, 19: 427.

16 *Notes*, 71.

Notes to Chapter Two, pages 22–32.

17 *Garden Book*, 12–13.

18 *Garden Book*, 16–17. This was no easy task in the dead of winter. Jefferson noted the conditions in a dispassionate manner, "a very cold snowy day which obliged them to be very often warming; under a cover of planks, so low, that in about half the work their stroke was not more than 2/3 of a good one."

19 TJ to William Hamilton, 1806, in Edwin M. Betts and Hazlehurst Bolton Perkins, *Thomas Jefferson's Flower Garden at Monticello* (Charlottesville: Thomas Jefferson Foundation, 1971), 1.

20 Le Duc de la Rochefoucauld-Liancour in Merrill D. Peterson, ed., *Visitors to Monticello* (Charlottesville: University Press of Virginia, 1989), 22.

21 TJ to Maria Cosway, October 12, 1786, *Papers*, 10: 443–53.

22 Margaret Bayard Smith in Peterson, *Visitors to Monticello*, 45.

23 Francis Calley Gray in Peterson, *Visitors to Monticello*, 57.

24 George Ticknor in Peterson, *Visitors to Monticello*, 61.

25 TJ Account Book, 1771, in *Garden Book*, 27.

26 Issac Jefferson, "Memoirs of a Monticello Slave," in James A. Bear, ed., *Jefferson at Monticello* (Charlottesville: University Press of Virginia, 1967), 21.

27 Byrd in Richard C. Beatty and William J. Mulloy, eds., *William Byrd's Natural History of Virginia or the Newly Discovered Eden* (Richmond, Virginia: Dietz Press, 1940), 54.

28 Robert Beverley, *The History and Present State of Virginia*, Book 2 (London, 1705), 37.

29 *Notes*, 158.

30 *Garden Book*, 15.

31 Susan Stein, *The Worlds of Thomas Jefferson at Monticello* (New York: H. N. Abrams and Charlottesville: The Thomas Jefferson Memorial Foundation, 1993).

32 Baron de Montlezun in Peterson, *Visitors to Monticello*, 68.

33 Ibid., 68–70.

34 TJ to Dr. Thomas Cooper, January 16, 1814, L&B, 14: 54–63.

35 A complete list of titles is given in E. Millicent Sowerby, ed., *Catalogue of the Library of Thomas Jefferson* (Washington, D.C.: Library of Congress, 1952–1959).

36 Among Jefferson's books on natural history were important volumes on plants, garden design, landscape design, and gardening, including Thomas Whately's *Observations on Modern Gardening*

(1770). Gronovius's edition of Clayton's *Flora Virginica* and Philip Miller's works have already been mentioned. The same books were extremely influential in the life and work of an English contemporary of Jefferson, the Rev. Gilbert White. White's *Natural History and Antiquities of Selborne in the County of Southampton* is filled with detailed observations on the natural history of southern England. Miller's *Kalendar* set out a framework for the lists, notes, and all the other observations of nature and gardening that White (and Jefferson) had typically collected. Like Jefferson, White kept a detailed weather record and noted the arrival and departure of migratory "birds of passage." Also like Jefferson he was interested in the new technique of vaccination against smallpox and urged it on the villagers.

Also important for Jefferson were copies of the latest books from England concerning experiments in agricultural practices, especially rotation of crops. His library eventually included a range of books from Richard Bradley's *A General Treatise of Husbandry and Gardening* (1724) to Arthur Young's *A Course in Experimental Agriculture* (1771) and *Rural Economy* (1773), and Nicholas Douette-Richardot's *Practique de l'Agriculture* (1806). See also: Joseph Ewan, "How Many Botany Books Did Jefferson Own?" *Bulletin of the Missouri Botanical Garden*, 64 (June 1976), unpaged.

Notes to Chapter Three, pages 33–42.

37 *Garden Book*, 33.
38 TJ to Dr. Vine Utley, March 21, 1819, L&B, 15: 186–88.
39 Karen Hess, ed., Mary Randolph, *The Virginia House-wife* (Columbia: University of South Carolina Press, 1984), 126, 128.
40 *Notes*, 58.
41 TJ to Abigail Adams, September 25, 1785, *Papers*, 8: 547–49.
42 *Garden Book*, 469.
43 TJ to Madame Noailles de Tessé, January 30, 1803, in *Garden Book*, 285.
44 For details of Jefferson's experiences with grapes, see Peter Hatch, *The Fruits and Fruit Trees of Monticello* (Charlottesville: University of Virginia Press, 1998).
45 Gerard W. Gawalt, "Jefferson's Slaves: Crop Accounts at Monticello, 1805–1808," *Journal of the Afro-American Historical and Genealogical Society*, 13 (1994): 19–38.
46 Andrea Wulf, *The Brother Gardeners: Botany, Empire and the Birth of an Obsession* (London: Heinemann, 2008).
47 Benjamin Smith Barton, *Transactions of the American Philosophical Society*, 3 (1793): 334–47.
48 TJ to Benjamin Rush, January 16, 1811, L&B, 13: 1–9.
49 TJ to Thomas Mann Randolph, January 1, 1792, *Papers*, 23: 7–8.
50 *Thomas Jefferson's Farm Book*, Edwin Morris Betts, ed. (Princeton: Princeton University Press, 1953), 45–46.
51 TJ to George Washington, June 28, 1793, *Papers*, 26: 396–98.
52 TJ to James Madison, June 29, 1793, *Papers*, 26: 401–4.
53 TJ to William Strickland, March 23, 1798, *Papers*, 30: 209–13.

Notes to Chapter Four, pages 43–53

54 Detailed discussions in Daniel J. Boorstin, *The Lost World of Thomas Jefferson* (Boston: Henry Holt, 1948) and John C. Greene, *American Science in the Age of Jefferson* (Ames: Iowa State University Press, 1984).

55 In 1791 Jefferson wrote to his friend Harry Innes, thanking him for having sent "information in the line of Natural History, and … political news. The first is my passion, the last my duty, and therefore both desirable." March 7, 1791, *Papers*, 19: 521–22.

56 In modern times, the term natural history has come to imply a sense of amateurishness and a distinction from "real" science. Bird watching is natural history and a bird watcher is a naturalist rather than a scientist. Ornithology, on the other hand (for example, discovering how birds navigate during migrations), is science.

57 John Bartram was responsible for introducing more than three hundred North American tree and plant species to Europe. See Joseph Kastner, *A Species of Eternity* (New York: Knopf, 1977).

58 Joseph Ewan and Nesta Dunn Ewan, *Benjamin Smith Barton: Naturalist and Physician in Jeffersonian America* (St. Louis: Missouri Botanical Garden Press, 2007).

59 TJ, "Notes on a Tour into the Southern Parts of France," 1787, *Papers*, 11: 442.

60 TJ to John Jay, May 4, 1787, *Papers*, 11: 339.

61 American Philosophical Society, "Circular on the Hessian Fly," April 17, 1791, *Papers*, 23: 430–32.

62 TJ to William Prince, July 6, 1791, *Papers*, 20: 603–4.

63 TJ to (Judge) William Johnson, May 10, 1817, *Garden Book*, 572.

64 TJ to Dr. John Manners, February 22, 1814, L&B, 14: 97–103.

65 Thomas Mann Randolph, Jr. to TJ, April, 14, 1787, *Papers*, 11: 291–92.

Notes to Chapter Five, pages 54–72

66 Barbé-Marbois' questionnaires were not all sent out on the same date. Jefferson's copy from Jones is dated October, 1780, and the reply from New Hampshire was written on December 10, 1780. The copy for Delaware, however, was sent on February 10, 1781.

67 Alexander Moore, "Thomas Bee's Notes on the State of South Carolina," *Journal of the Early Republic* 7 (1987): 115–22.

68 John Witherspoon, "A Description of the State of New-Jersey. Answers in Part to Mr. Marbois's Questions Respecting New-Jersey," in *The Miscellaneous Works of the Rev. John Witherspoon*, vol. 4 (Philadelphia, 1803), 303–12.

69 Otis G. Hammond, ed., "Gen. Sullivan's Description of New Hampshire to the Marquis de Marbois. Letters and Papers of Major-General John Sullivan, Continental Army," *Collections of the New Hampshire Historical Society*, 1779–1795, vol. 3 (Concord, New Hampshire, 1939): 229–39.

70 TJ to D'Anmours, November 30, 1780, *Papers*, 4: 167–68.

71 William Peden, ed., *Notes on the State of Virginia*, Introduction (Chapel Hill: University of North Carolina Press, 1955).

72 Beverley had divided his book into four parts: The history of the First Settlement of *Virginia*, and the Government thereof, to the present Time; The Natural Productions and Conveniencies of the Country, suited to Trade and Improvement; The Native *Indians*, their Religion, Laws, and Customs, in War and Peace; and The present State of the Country, as to the Polity of the Government, and the Improvements of the Land.

73 James C. Kelly and William M. S. Rasmussen, *The Virginia Landscape: A Cultural History* (Charlottesville: Howell Press, 2000).

74 TJ to Samuel Brown, July 14, 1813, L&B, 13: 310–12.

75 *Notes*, 40. In his section on the pecan Jefferson showed his thorough knowledge of the work of "Don Ulloa," remarking that the latter had called the tree "Pacanos."

76 *Notes*, 48.

77 *Notes*, 267. and Georges Louis Leclerc, Comte de Buffon, *Histoire Naturelle, Générale et Particulière*,

vol. 9 (Paris: L'Imprimierie Royale, 1761), 101–8 (the first edition, quarto). Buffon further expounded on his Theory of Degeneracy in volume 14, 1766. (Volume numbers and dates for editions of Buffon vary. In the duodecimo edition used by Jefferson the reference is to volume 18: 100–46.)

78 TJ to Marquis de Chastellux, June 7, 1785, *Papers*, 8: 184–86.

79 Peter Kalm, *En Resa til Norra America* (1753–1761); English translation *Travels into North America* (London, 1770).

80 Byrd in Beatty and Mulloy, *William Byrd's Natural History of Virginia*, 18.

81 De Pauw in Henry Steele Commager and Giordanetti Elmo, *Was America a Mistake? An Eighteenth-Century Controversy* (New York: Harper, 1967), 83.

82 Ibid., 77.

83 C. Vann Woodward, *The Old World's New World* (New York: Oxford University Press, 1991).

84 Buffon, *Histoire Naturelle*, 9 (1761), 101–2; *Supplementary Volume* 4 (1777), 532–35.

85 Jefferson listed a number of comparable theories in a letter to Adams (May 27, 1813). They included as ancestors of the Indians: the ancient Greeks (with Indians speaking Hebrew), "soldiers sent by Kouli Kahan to conquer Japan;" the Tartars (who also brought the wolf, bear and fox) via Noah's ark having landed in Asia; and the Persians. There was even a theory that God created Adam and Eve in America.

86 Buffon, *Histoire Naturelle*, vol. 9, 114.

87 Ibid., 54–61.

88 W.D. I. Rolfe, "William Hunter (1718–1783) on Irish 'elk' and Stubb's Moose," *Archives of Natural History*, 11 (1983): 263–90.

89 TJ to Archibald Carey, January 7, 1786, *Papers*, 9: 158–59.

90 TJ to John Sullivan, October 5, 1787, *Papers*, 12: 208–9.

91 Joseph Ellis, *American Sphinx, the Character of Thomas Jefferson* (New York: Knopf, 1997), 99.

92 TJ to Buffon, Paris, October 1, 1887, *Papers*, 12: 194–95.

93 Ibid.

94 TJ to John Sullivan, October 5, 1787, *Papers*, 12: 208–9.

95 F. Webster, ed., *The Private Correspondence of Daniel Webster*, vol. 1 (Boston, 1857), 371.

96 In George Ticknor Curtis, *The Life of Daniel Webster* (New York: Appleton, 1889), 587.

97 John Robert Moore, "Goldsmith's Degenerate Song-birds: an Eighteenth-Century Fallacy in Ornithology," *Isis*, 34 (Spring, 1943): 324–27.

98 *Notes*, 69; 70–71.

99 *Notes*, 68–69.

Notes to Chapter Six, pages 73–89

100 Keith Thomson, *The Legacy of the Mastodon* (New Haven: Yale University Press, 2008).

101 An Extract of Several Letters from Cotton Mather, D.D., to John Woodward, M.D. and Richard Waller, *Philosophical Transactions of the Royal Society*, 29 (1714): 62–71.

102 John W. Jordon, ed., "Journal of James Kenny, 1761–1763," *Pennsylvania Magazine of History and Biography*, 37 (1913): 163.

103 Ibid., 180.

104 Peter Kalm in John Reinhold Forster, ed., *Travels into North America* (Barre, Massachusetts: Imprint Society, 1972), 365. The French edition of Kalm was published in 1761 and the first English edition in 1772.

105 Franklin to l'Abbe Chapppe d'Auteroche, Jan 31, 1768, in William Wilcox, ed., *The Papers of Benjamin Franklin*, 15 (New Haven: Yale University Press, 1972), 33–34.

106 Paul Semonin, *American Monster* (New York: New York University Press, 2000).

107 Among those from whom Jefferson had requested information for *Notes* was Yale University President Ezra Stiles. Disconcertingly, Stiles wrote back with lots of references to huge fossil bones, but he thought that they all belonged to a bipedal giant that was definitely extinct. Stiles to TJ, June 21, 1784, *Papers*, 7: 312–17.

108 *Notes*, 55.

109 *Notes*, 46.

110 George Turner, "Memoir on the Extraneous Fossils Designed to Show that They Are the Remains of More than One Species of Non-descript Animal," *Transactions of the American Philosophical Society*, 4 (1799): 510–18.

111 G. G. Goodwin, "The First Living Elephant in America," *Journal of Mammalogy*, 6 (1925): 256–63.

112 Mark Catesby, *The Natural History of Florida, Carolina and the Bahama Islands*, 2 (London, 1843), Appendix, vii.

113 *Notes*, 45.

114 *Notes*, 46.

115 *Notes*, 47.

116 *Notes*, 55.

117 Nicholas Collin, "An Essay on Those Inquiries in Natural Philosophy, Which at Present Are Most Beneficial to the United States of North America," *Transactions of the American Philosophical Society*, 3 (1793): iii–xxvii.

118 *Transactions of the American Philosophical Society*, 4 (1799): xxxvii–xxxix.

119 John Adams to F. A. van der Kemp, January 26, 1802, in Edward Handler, "'Nature Itself Is All Arcanum': the Scientific Outlook of John Adams," *Proceedings of the American Philosophical Society*, 120 (1976): 216–29.

120 John Stuart to TJ, April 11, 1796, *Papers*, 29: 64–65.

121 TJ to Archibald Stuart, May 26, 1796, *Papers*, 29: 113.

122 TJ to Benjamin Rush, January 22, 1797, *Papers*, 29: 275.

123 Thomas Jefferson, "A Memoir on the Discovery of Certain Bones of a Quadruped of the Clawed Kind in the Western Parts of Virginia," *Transactions of the American Philosophical Society*, 4 (1799): 246–60.

124 *The Monthly Magazine and British Register*, vol. 2 (1796): 637–38.

125 William Carmichael to TJ, January 26, 1789, *Papers*, 14: 498–505.

126 Julian Boyd, "The Megalonyx, the Megatherium, and Thomas Jefferson's Lapse of Memory," *Proceedings of the American Philosophical Society*, 102 (1958): 420–35.

127 The specimen was actually from Lujan, Argentina. The best description of its discovery and description is in G.G. Simpson, *Discoverers of the Lost World* (New Haven: Yale University Press, 1984), 3–12.

128 TJ to Caspar Wistar, February 3, 1801, *Papers*, 32: 544–45.

129 George Gaylord Simpson and H. Tobien, "The Rediscovery of Peale's Mastodon," *Proceedings of the American Philosophical Society*, 98 (1954): 279–81.

130 Benjamin Smith Barton, "Letter to M. Cuvier, of Paris," *Philadelphia Medical and Physical Journal*, 3 (first supplement, 1808): 22–35.

131 TJ to George Rogers Clark, January 6, 1783, *Papers*, 6: 218–19.

132 TJ to Caspar Wistar, March 20, 1808, L&B, 12: 15–16.

133 Ibid.

134 Caspar Wistar, "An Account of Two Heads, Found in the Morass, Called the Big Bone Lick, and Presented to the Society, by Mr. Jefferson," *Transactions of the American Philosophical Society*, new series, vol. 1 (1809): 375–80.

135 Baron de Montlezun, *Voyage fait dans les années 1816 et 1817 de New York a la Nouvelle-Orleans* (Paris 1818) in J. M. Carriere and L.G. Moffatt, "A Frenchman Visits Albemarle, 1816," *Papers of the Albemarle County Historical Society*, 4 (1944): 39–55; Peterson, *Visitors to Monticello*, 67.

Notes to Chapter Seven, pages 90–95

136 Eugene R. Sheridan, *Jefferson and Religion* (Charlottesville, Virginia: Thomas Jefferson Foundation, 1998).

137 While he was in France he learned of a French "savant," M. de la Sauvagiere, a man Jefferson considered to be "overcharged with imagination," who swore that he had watched shells growing unconnected with animal bodies and had once "made a collection of shells for the Emperor's cabinet." Jefferson concluded that this was "not against any law of nature and is therefore possible: but it is so little analogous to her habitual processes that, if true, it would be extraordinary...." "Notes from Tour through Southern France," *Papers*, 11: 460–61.

138 J.P. Richter, *The Literary Works of Leonardo da Vinci*, vol. 2, 2nd Edition (Cambridge: Oxford University Press, 1939), 175.

139 Ibid.

140 Thomas Burnet, *Telluria Theoria Sacra: the Sacred Theory of the Earth* (1681, 1684), trans. & ed. Basil Willey (Londona: Centaur Press, 1965): 196–97.

141 TJ to Charles Thomson, Paris, December 17, 1786, *Papers*, 10: 608–9. See John Whitehurst, *An Inquiry into the Original System and Formation of the Earth* (London, 1778).

142 Benjamin Franklin, "Conjectures Concerning the Formation of the Earth," *Transactions of the American Philosophical Society*, 3 (1793): 1–5.

143 These were probably Silurian-age brachiopod shells.

144 Rev. James Madison to TJ, December 28, 1786, *Papers*, 10: 642–44. Reverend Madison was cousin to the future fourth president.

145 TJ to David Rittenhouse, January 25, 1786, *Papers*, 9: 215–17.

146 TJ to Charles Thomson, December 17, 1786, *Papers*, 10: 608–9.

147 TJ to Charles Thomson, April 20, 1787, *Papers*, 12: 159–66.

148 TJ to C.F.C. de Volney, February 8, 1805, L&B, 11: 62–69.

149 TJ to Dr. John P. Emmett, May 2, 1826, L&B, 16: 168–72.

Notes to Chapter Eight, pages 96–108

150 De Pauw, *Was America a Mistake?*, 81; Buffon, *Histoire Naturelle*, 9 (1761): 106–7.

151 *Notes*, 67–68.

152 Jefferson provided a lengthy documentation of the Chresap affair in an appendix to *Notes*. See also, discussion in Anthony Wallace, *Jefferson and the Indians* (Cambridge: Harvard University Press, 1999), chapter 1.

153 Edward Seeber, "Chief Logan's Speech in France," *Modern Language Notes*, 61: 412–16.

154 Buffon, *Histoire Naturelle*, 9 (1761): 104. Translation in *Notes*, 306.

155 TJ to John Adams, June 11, 1812, L&B, 13: 156–61.

156 Louis B Wright, ed., *The Prose Works of William Byrd of Westover* (Cambridge: Harvard University Press, 1966), 160.

157 Witherspoon, *The Miscellaneous Works*, 312.

158 *Notes*, 98–103.

159 Beverley, *The History and Present State of Virginia*, Book 3, 1.

160 TJ to Chastellux, June 7, 1785, *Papers*, 8: 185.

161 Ibid.

162 Kalm, *Travels into North America*, 365. Kalm had written of Europeans in America that no one "born in this country, should live to be eighty or ninety years of age ... In the last war it plainly appeared that [the] new Americans were by far less hardy than the Europeans ... the women cease bearing children sooner than in Europe."

163 Buffon, "Addition a l'article des Variétes de l'espèce humain, Des Americains," *Histoire Naturelle*, *Supplementary Volume*, 4 (1777): 530–31.

164 TJ to James Madison, January 1, 1784, *Papers*, 6: 436–38.

165 Estimates of the age of the earth at that time already diverged far from the traditional six thousand years, calculated from internal Biblical evidence. Some scholars thought the earth was many hundreds of thousands of years old, others were already talking in terms of millions.

166 TJ to Benjamin Smith Barton, September 21, 1809, *Retirement Series* 1: 555–57.

167 *Notes*, 106.

168 It is not fair to Jefferson to expect him to have been a paragon of all the virtues, when he was necessarily very much a man of his time. Nonetheless there is an irony in this last statement which, as modern scientific methodology seems to have shown, was contradicted by his later behavior. See Eugene A. Foster, et al., "Jefferson fathered slave's last child," *Nature, 396 (1998): 27–28.*

169 Samuel Stanhope Smith, *An Essay on the Causes of the Variety of Complexion and Figure in the Human Species ...* (Philadelphia: Sampson and Co., 1810).

Notes to Chapter Nine, pages 109–20

170 TJ to George Rogers Clark, December 4, 1783, *Papers*, 6: 371.

171 Paul Russell Cutright, *Contributions of Philadelphia to Lewis and Clark History* (Philadelphia: Lewis and Clark Heritage Trail Foundation, 2001).

172 Jefferson immediately sent out a second expedition, under General Zebulon Pike, to explore "Louisiana" and the Missouri basin in Kansas and Arkansas. They reached westward as far as Colorado. On the way home, they got lost and were arrested as spies by the Spanish militia at a fort they had built near Santa Fe.

173 TJ to Meriwether Lewis, June 20, 1803, in Donald Jackson, ed., *Letters of the Lewis and Clark Expedition, vol. 1* (Urbana: University of Illinois Press, 1978), 61–66.

174 Robert J. Miller, *Native America, Discovered and Conquered: Thomas Jefferson, Lewis and Clark, and Manifest Destiny* (Westport, Connecticut: Praeger, 2006), 72.

175 TJ to Albert Gallatin, January 7, 1808, L&B, 11: 415–16.

176 Miller, *Native America*, 71.

177 Gary Moulton, ed., *The Journals of the Lewis & Clark Expedition*, vol. 3 (Lincoln: University of Nebraska Press, 1987), 330.

178 Bil Gilbert, "The Incredible Odyssey of the President's Beasts," *Audubon*, 91 (1989): 110.

179 James L. Reveal, et al., "The Lewis and Clark Collections of Vascular Plants: Names, Types, and Comments," *Proceedings of the Academy of Natural Sciences of Philadelphia*, 149 (1999): 1–64. H. Wayne Phillips, *Plants of the Lewis and Clark Expedition* (Missoula: Montana Press Publishing Company, 2003).

180 Paul Russell Cutright, *Lewis & Clark, Pioneering Naturalists* (Urbana: University of Illinois Press, 1969).

181 Peter Hatch, "'Public Treasures': Thomas Jefferson and the Garden Plants of Lewis and Clark," *Twinleaf Journal*, 2003.

182 Wallace, *Jefferson and the Indians*, 106.

183 Paul Allen, ed., *History of the expedition under the Command of Captains Lewis and Clark, to the sources of the Missouri, thence across the Rocky mountains and down the river Columbia to the Pacific ocean* (Philadelphia: Bradford and Inskeep, 1814).

184 Castle McLaughlin, *Arts of Diplomacy: Lewis and Clark's Indian Collection* (Seattle: University of Washington Press, 2003); Wallace, *Jefferson and the Indians*, 106.

185 Robert Cox, "'I never yet parted': Bernard McMahon and the Seeds of the Corps of Discovery," *Transactions of the American Philosophical Society*, 94 (2004): 102–35.

186 Richard McCourt and Earl Spamer, *Jefferson's Botanists: Lewis and Clark Discover the Plants of the West* (Philadelphia: Academy of Natural Sciences, 2004.).

Notes to Chapter Ten, pages 121–25

187 Ellis, *American Sphinx*, 99.

188 Charles E. Miller, *Jefferson and Nature, an Interpretation* (Baltimore: The Johns Hopkins University Press, 1993).

189 Ellis, *American Sphinx*, 37.

190 *Notes*, 170.

191 TJ to John Jay, August 23, 1785, *Papers*, 8: 426–28.

192 Maurizio Valsania, "'Our Original Barbarism': Man vs. Nature in Thomas Jefferson's Moral Experience," *Journal of the History of Ideas*, 65 (2004): 627–45.

Index

About the Monticello Monograph Series

This series, launched to commemorate the 250th anniversary of Jefferson's birth on April 13, 1993, consists of publications of enduring value on various aspects of Jefferson's diverse interests and legacy.

Also in print and currently available:

THOMAS JEFFERSON: A BRIEF BIOGRAPHY
by Dumas Malone

THE POLITICAL WRITINGS OF THOMAS JEFFERSON
edited by Merrill D. Peterson

SLAVERY AT MONTICELLO
by Lucia Stanton

JEFFERSON'S BOOKS
by Douglas L. Wilson

ARCHAEOLOGY AT MONTICELLO
by William M. Kelso

JEFFERSON AND RELIGION
by Eugene R. Sheridan

FREE SOME DAY: THE AFRICAN-AMERICAN FAMILIES OF MONTICELLO
by Lucia Stanton

JEFFERSON'S WEST: A JOURNEY WITH LEWIS AND CLARK
by James P. Ronda

THE LEVY FAMILY AND MONTICELLO 1834-1923:
SAVING THOMAS JEFFERSON'S HOUSE
by Melvin I. Urofsky

JEFFERSON AND SCIENCE
by Silvio A. Bedini

LETTERS FROM THE HEAD AND HEART: WRITINGS OF THOMAS JEFFERSON
by Andrew Burstein

JEFFERSON AND MONROE: CONSTANT FRIENDSHIP AND RESPECT
by Noble E. Cunningham, Jr.

THE LOUISIANA PURCHASE: JEFFERSON'S NOBLE BARGAIN?
by James E. Lewis, Jr.

JEFFERSON AND EDUCATION
by Jennings L. Wagoner, Jr.